Branchising

Proven
Techniques for
Rapid Company
Expansion
and
Market Dominance

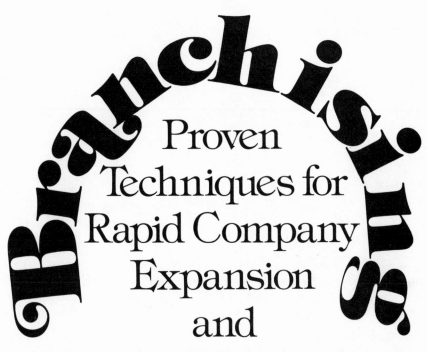

Proven Techniques for Rapid Company Expansion and Market Dominance

David D. Seltz

President
Seltz Franchising Developments, Inc.

McGraw-Hill Book Co.

New York   St. Louis   San Francisco   Auckland
Bogotá   Singapore   Johannesburg   London
Madrid   Mexico   Montreal   New Delhi
Panama   São Paulo   Hamburg
Sydney   Tokyo   Paris
Toronto

Library of Congress Cataloging in Publication Data
Seltz, David D
  Branchising.

  Includes index.
  1. Branches (Business enterprises) I. Title.
HD38.S394   658.8'706   79-19549
ISBN 0-07-056215-6

1234567890   DODO   89876543210

The editors for this book were W. Hodson Mogan, William
R. Newton, Joan Matthews; the designer was Mark E. Safran;
and the production supervisor was Sally Fliess. It was set in
Roma by ComCom.

It was printed and bound by the R. R. Donnelley and Sons
Company.

Contents

Preface

The Need

Business today is facing new problems, requiring fresh approaches and new dynamic decisions. Traditional precepts have undergone drastic changes. There is now a need for accelerated expansion to help achieve effective market penetration. Multiple branches must be established, almost simultaneously. To remain stationary is to retrogress.

This need for rapid branch expansion—and I stress the word "rapid"—is particularly urgent during inflationary periods. The excessive costs of doing business make it difficult for the "small," single-unit business to survive. Profit margins constrict, and it becomes necessary to increase the number of profit margins or individual profit centers to help achieve a desirable "net" . . . and to do so as quickly as possible. Branching helps to achieve this—effectively.

Rapid achievement of multiple branches—in most markets throughout the country —has been an underlying factor in the success of the reigning retail "giants"—the McDonalds's the Radio Shacks, the Pizza Huts, the Burger Kings, and others.

How This Book Can Help

Use this book as an "idea activator," to help develop new options—new and better ways to do what is being done now. Use it to help develop new profit centers as a result of recognizing current trends; to help achieve an "overview" of the business, while avoiding the highly expensive trial-and-error route toward profits; and importantly, to avoid "Farmer Ezra's Cow Syndrome." To elucidate: Farmer Ezra's cow made a cowpath. . . . The cowpath grew into a road . . . into other roads . . . and eventually an entire city was built around the cowpath . . . around an original plan created by a cow. . . . But no one ever questioned the origin or validity of the original plan!

The Scope of the Book

This book not only describes the concepts needed for successful business expansion and "branching out" but also presents a complete plan for implementing a Branchise program. The book is intended for the manager involved in the growth of his organization—the company executive, the corporate planner, the director of marketing, the finance manager, the company attorney or accountant, and in fact, any business executive seeking to achieve innovativeness and add on profits. And today's individual entrepreneur, with the motivation and financial backing to enter into a viable business, can use this book as a blueprint for creating and expanding his own enterprise.

You may have noticed my use of the masculine pronoun "his" when referring to the business manager and the entrepreneur in a general sense. I am fully aware that women are currently playing important roles in business and are actively assuming positions of responsibility that used to be held almost exclusively by men. Unfortunately, our language has not kept pace with social changes, and there is as yet no set of third-person pronouns that refer equally to men and women. Because of the current limitations of our vocabulary, therefore, in this book I have used the masculine pronouns when referring to individuals in a general, "generic" sense; I hope my readers will regard such references as applying both to women and to men.

David D. Seltz

Part ONE

The Concept

The Need

WHAT IS BRANCHISING?

Branchising is a generic term covering a myriad of company expansion methods. It's a concept geared to today's economic needs that helps a company:

1. To "branch out," achieving *rapid market dominance*
2. To achieve multiple retail branches with *minimal capital outlay* through use of the OPM principle (other people's money)
3. To receive *immediate and ongoing cash flow*—in the form of an initial training and establishment fee, and continuing royalties
4. And most important, to attract, and acquire, top-level, *highly qualified managers,* individuals who have *invested* their own money in the business and are dedicated and entrepreneurial in outlook and accomplishment: excellent personnel standards not normally available from *salaried employees*

Pseudo-Partnership Concept

Central to the concept of Branchising is some form of "pseudo-partnership." Here, both the parent and the operator share in the business, relative to their respective capital contributions, with the operator often able to acquire a subsequent larger share, based on future earnings and predesignated performance standards. This policy provides the small entrepreneur with an incentive plus ownership of his own business based on a minimum investment. It provides an important "built-in" growth element and links the parent and operator together as a "team," mutually striving for profits.

Marketing Concept

In a broader sense, Branchising is a system of marketing or distribution built around the licensing to individuals or groups of the right to do business under the auspices of a parent company. "Branchisees" (branch operators) thus receive the benefit of its name, product, prestige, experience, system, and procedure, with both "Branchisor" (parent company) and Branchisee maintaining their status as independent persons.

ONE

Instant Capital Concept

Involvement of local capital is the basic tenet of Branchising, and with involved energies harnessed and motivation maximized, local representation is as interested in sales and success as the parent company. Branchising offers instant capital. While the investment of capital is the key to motivation, it also means minimum capital outlay for the company wishing to expand operations, sales, and distribution. Thus, expansion is faster. Higher sales levels mean greater efficiencies. Faster, greater earnings mean more funds available for the other needs of the growing corporation without costly borrowing charges or dilution of equity.

Instant Manpower Concept

Branchising offers instant manpower. It relieves strain on a corporation's capital structure and lessens the strain on essential manpower. Branch investors also invest their time and talent to make the local business a success. This source of serious, interested, highly motivated manpower is a great and invaluable asset. It is readily available in suitable quantity and quality because of the unique attractions and rewards of the Branchising system.

TEN ADVANTAGES OF EXPANDING THROUGH BRANCHISING

Potential marketing advantages of Branchising are indicated by the following:

1. Expansion rate can be controlled. By merely adjusting various budget segments, the Branchisor can assign Branchisees as rapidly or as slowly as desired.
2. Expansion of the company's activities is financed by the branch operators. After a relatively few Branchisees are sold, the entire company program becomes self-liquidating.
3. Profits are increased without the necessity of a comparable increase in overhead and capital investment.
4. Administrative efficiency is significantly improved through manualized operating, sales, and training procedures.
5. Knowledge and skills gained by company and management are more fully capitalized on.
6. The branch operator's investment "locks him in," guaranteeing his devotion to the success of his business.
7. The overall operation will enjoy a competitive advantage and greater profits as a result of increased selling power.
8. A vehicle is provided for the retention and more profitable utilization of key personnel within the parent organization.

2

9. Branchisees are provided with a flow of sales promotion material, and the parent operation enjoys the benefit of superior advertising not economically feasible if done by individual effort.

10. Through the creation of uniform operating, training, and sales procedures, the parent operation is usually improved.

Achieves Intensive Use of Capital

A basic objective of any branch expansion program is the more intensive use of capital. Generally speaking, higher working capital turnover supports a higher volume of sales. The various methods of corporate expansion considered herein have, as their objective, both higher working capital velocity and the increase of present working capital, without increasing equity participation. These methods may involve de facto business "partners" or indirect contributors to working capital.

OPM Principal of Financing

While quickened expansion constitutes a formidable program, perhaps not financially achievable under ordinary circumstances, it can become possible through selective use of the "OPM principle."

OPM is a respected technique of the bankers—it is "other people's money." The traditional OPM approach has been the borrowing of funds or the realization of monies by the public sale of equity. However, most of the financing techniques considered in this book will involve funds developed from the distribution system, itself, and the way in which it is financed.

Economies of Scale

Since more units, or profit centers, would be created, additional economies of scale would accrue to all parties. These would include economies in purchasing goods, supplies, and outside services such as advertising and insurance, as well as the opportunity to expand internal production and promotional facilities.

Easier to Raise Capital

With an expanded operation, investors (institutional or private) will generally look favorably upon the company in terms of loaned or equity capital. For a public company, a new opportunity presents itself: the opportunity to buy back for stock one of its successful Branchises and pool its earnings into the parent, thereby showing greater earnings for its stock. Thus, the remaining stock may grow in value offsetting the shares traded.

SUMMATION OF BRANCHISING OBJECTIVES

The major aims of a Branchising program are:

1. To activate branch profit centers as rapidly as is consistent with sound business practice

2. To establish a branch network consisting of individual operators having the ability to achieve maximum potential from their market area while contributing to the overall enhancement of the parent company image

3. To formulate a program which will be self-liquidating at a predetermined point and, thereafter, become self-sustaining and profitable for the parent company

4. To develop this branch program without disrupting the existing company to dealer relationship

EARNINGS SOURCES OF BRANCHISING

Branchising programs act to generate earnings "flow" from a variety of possible sources and services:

1. From a percentage of gross sales in the form of a "royalty" or other payment arrangement. Thus, the greater the sales volume the greater the potential earnings of the parent company.

2. From a prescribed minimum fee paid periodically, e.g., weekly or monthly. This minimum fee is projected to provide an adequate profit for the parent's continuing services. Some agreements also specify "a percentage or a minimum," whichever is greater.

3. From sales of products or services. In this instance the Branchisor may have a unique product, minimally affected by competition, and is satisfied with the potential profits obtainable from product sales, thus waiving other possible fees.

4. From leasing or rental fees. These are derived on a continuing basis from rental of equipment, property, and other assets.

5. From specialized services furnished to Branchisees. Such services include advertising placement, training, computerization, record-keeping, management consultation, etc.

6. Branch operation renewal fee. This is stipulated in the contract.

Difference between Franchising and Branchising

Franchising is one—but only one—market expansion concept within the umbrella term "Branchising." There are, of course, many points of similarity between the two concepts. In each instance there is an entrepreneurial association based on mutual written commitments. The branch operator makes an investment and seeks to achieve equity interest and self-ownership.

4

Branchising differs from franchising to the extent that it offers *options.* Many of these options may tend to bypass some of the regulations now confronting franchising. Other options may offer a more selective, pinpointed approach toward the more effective implementation of a particular business. In some instances Branchising may also refer to collateral factors of business operation, e.g., more effective sales, management, and administrative techniques, etc., that can achieve added profit dimensions ("centers") for a business.

At the very least, Branchising can open many innovative "doorways" for any business and help to achieve effective and accelerated market penetration. It can trigger highly valuable primary or secondary solutions to many types of current business problems.

TODAY'S BUSINESS STATUS

Here are some of today's economic problems that necessitate branchising:

Voracious competition

Heavy advertising costs

High operating expenses, low net profit[1]

Personnel mobility (requires heavy replacement costs)

Regulatory constraints

New consumer trends (require new business orientations)

Inability to survive as a single unit

[1]A recent article commented that a franchised hamburger chain was taking measures to offset "surge in costs and competition." A similar thrust has characterized most other businesses.

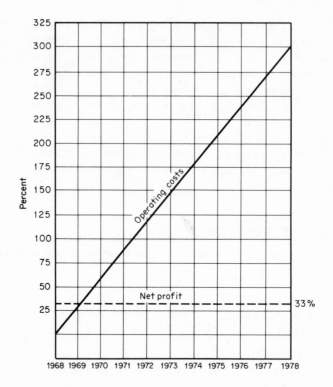

Figure 1-1 This chart exemplifies the general relationship between rising costs (which have steady upward mobility) and "profit percentage" that remains stationery. This points to the imperativeness of Branchising—the attainment of multiple net profits from multiple branch units.

New Trends

FOURTEEN ECONOMIC "TRENDS" INFLUENCING NEED FOR BRANCH EXPANSION

The trends summarized in the following pages reflect the changes in economic conditions, marketing receptivity, and consumer attitudes that influence today's urgent need for Branchising techniques.

These trends have developed gradually and, today, constitute a highly visible reality. They demand awareness and serious consideration on the part of business.

Consider these trends as both a *caution* and an *opportunity*. The cautions point out dangers that may impede your business progress today. The opportunities provide vehicles to expedite quick expansion of a business and to help achieve increased penetration of the marketplace.

These trends include the following:

1. PERSONNEL MOBILITY

Today, *personnel turnover,* with the consequent loss of both experienced personnel and training investment, is a major profit deterrent, especially for non-Branchised organizations. For example, one organization with 1200 stores estimated that managerial personnel "turned over" once each 6 months. Furthermore, the company estimated that it cost an average of $2000 each to replace and retrain the new management. Multiplying this loss by 1200 units results in a loss of $2,400,000 in 6 months, or $4,800,000 in hidden annual losses, not readily apparent in a reading of the company's financial statements.

This example is not atypical. It reflects the experience of many—in fact, the majority—of larger people-intensive organizations. Such constant personnel turnover, especially on management levels, also affects the store's image and customer relations.

Table 2-1 shows how the investment loss for an employee leaving a company is calculated.

TABLE 2-1. Estimated Investment Loss for Each Employee Leaving from a Company at End of One Year

Hiring and terminating expense	$ 100
Training cost	1,000
Annual average salary	9,000
Benefits (insurance, holidays, etc.)	2,600
Estimate of total lost investment	$12,700

Based on average turnover of 30% annually for a staff of 1000, this could total $4 million yearly, not even including lost sales through employee turnover and loss of business image (based on constant managerial change, etc.).

2. ADVANTAGES OF ENTREPRENEURIAL MANAGEMENT

Entrepreneurial management, as contrasted with salaried employees, appears to offer more stability. It helps to achieve dedicated, "locked-in" managerial personnel who are strongly motivated toward the equity and independence offered by self-employment.

As one example, a research project was undertaken for a prominent chain of 5-and-10-type variety stores, to determine whether or not their 2000 stores could be more profitable independently owned rather than company-owned. For this purpose, fourteen units were selected for testing. These stores had reported annual losses ranging between $15,000 and $50,000. The test results showed that if each store were independently owned and managed, under some sort of "branch" contract, it could become a corporate asset and contribute an average of $25,000 per annum per unit to parent earnings, while yielding satisfactory profits to the local operator based on expanded sales and achieved economies.

3. POPULATION MOBILITY

voracious

With chains, conglomerates, and discount stores all competing for the consumer dollar, today's competition is not only dynamic, it is voracious. It can readily consume the small entrepreneur who cannot match its financial clout, management, and promotional sophistication. Neighborhood loyalty is a thing of the past. By means of the automobile, consumers gravitate toward the "big," regional shopping centers that are able to present the greatest variety of inventory and merchandising know-how to the potential buyer.

itinerant

This consumer mobility factor may, in fact, require a thorough reappraisal of a business to assure that it is geared to meet ensuing needs. It also requires maximum advertising exposure—and constant name and message impacts—to repetitively attract this itinerant customer.

Consumer mobility may also point up new, potentially profitable fields. For example, the resurgence of automotive aftermarket parts and services may suggest some aspect as a possible secondary business. Drive-ins have proliferated, indicating a new direction in site selection. Parking facilities have also become more and more important.

4. GREATER CAPITAL REQUIREMENTS

Greater initial capital investment and working capital are required for entry into today's business. Market penetration cannot be effected with minimum capital. Statistics show that the main cause of business failure is that of insufficient capital with which to reach the break-even point. The self-financing factor, characteristic of Branchising, helps to assure adequate cash flow on a continuing basis.

Branchising is capital-intensive. It operates on the OPM principle; hence, there is built-in, ongoing cash flow.

It is axiomatic that no matter how large and apparently prosperous an organization may be, it should seek the use of "other people's money" to avoid distillation of its own capital and to assure continued corporate liquidity.

5. NEED FOR INNOVATION

It's imperative that business recognize and respond to the continuous shifting of consumer receptivity and to other business changes. This requires innovativeness. Change is constant: What was suitable and adequate yesterday is often no longer appropriate today. There is a constant need to recognize and respond to changes, to modify or add on new products and services that can amplify sales potential and refurbish the corporate image.

Innovation is recognized as a "must" by most businesses. It is reflected in constant changes in decor, products, locations, services, promotions—in fact, in practically every aspect of the business. To keep constantly abreast of changes, successful businesses maintain active, highly expensive research and development departments and conduct constant field surveys (among both consumer and dealers). Businesses today recognize the need for innovativeness and seek to take initiatives before their competitors do.

Here are a few examples of innovativeness:

Catalog Corners. A catalog corner, a designated "corner" or area within an existing business (that features a catalog plus pertinent order forms), was recently introduced by J. C. Penney within Thrifty Drug Stores and other eligible locations. While avoiding the usual operating costs, these corners multiplied the number of available sales and profit centers.

Expanded Menus. A doughnut chain, faced with growing competition from coffee shops featuring fresh-baked donuts, expanded its menu to out-compete the coffee shops by offering such added items as soups, chili, frozen pastry, meat pies, etc. This innovative thrust has helped to significantly boost sales volume.

Expanded menus have been espoused by more and more restaurant chains as a means of achieving innovativeness and increasing profits without commensurately increasing expenses. Both Pizza Hut and McDonald's have been expanding their menu selections. Sambo's restaurants have also expanded their dinner-trade menu to attract an increased number of dinner patrons.

6. ATTAINING DIVERSIFICATION

Diversification is required not only as an offset to rising overhead but also to:

Keep pace with competition

Introduce additional profit centers which will produce income by a more intensive utilization of overhead

Protect markets by helping to prevent customer erosion because of a failure to recognize changed consumer receptivity

Even such a well-established, single-product company as McDonald's has recognized the need for product diversification. In addition to the standard fare of hamburgers and fried potatoes, McDonald's has tested salad bars, sundaes, and even meat pies. Also, the recent breakfast "add-on" has "smoothed" the traffic curve and created a new profit center, merely by using the same overhead more intensively. The company has indicated that this diversification program was necessary in order to offset nonproductive overhead, protect its prior market, and open new profit potentials.

Other examples of diversification follow:

1. J. C. Penney has conducted such disparate businesses as auto services, restaurants, supermarkets, and gas stations.

2. Supermarkets, recognizing the new economic influences and reduced patronage resulting from "women at work" (it is estimated that one out of five women, today, work at a job or their own business), have taken steps to offset the business decline caused by more families eating out. They have, in many instances, established fast-food restaurants as a corollary to their existing business. They have also given greater emphasis to the sale of nonfood lines, e.g., drugs.

3. Department stores have realized that since women at work have less time to shop, they seek to purchase all their day's needs within one establishment, if possible. To meet this demand, department stores have added many new services. Sears, Roebuck, for example, even provides baby sitters.

4. A California business called Merchant of Venice offered these diverse businesses within one establishment: an antique store, a furniture store, and a restaurant. The diner is thus able to buy any of the other items in the shop. The customer traffic in each of the businesses attracts patronage to the others.

10

5. Holiday Inns, too, is diversifying, and has recently introduced free-standing restaurants.

7. ATTAINING AN EXPANDED TABLE OF ORGANIZATION

It is clear that more personnel are required to support multiple company units. In addition to administrative staff, an extensive field staff is also required. These call for substantial ongoing expenditures. As an offset to these expenses, revenues from multiple branches are a necessity to finance and support an expanded table of organization.

An adequate table of organization and effective marketing support are interlinked. Each is a requirement of the other in order to achieve success. Hence, the acceleration/expansion within a minimum time span—made possible by Branchising—is important. An expanded table of organization resultantly becomes affordable.

8. NEED TO UPGRADE

It's axiomatic that, today, no business can afford to maintain the status quo. That permits a "vacuum" which becomes economically abhorrent.

The company that doesn't go forward is slipping backward. Competition and other dynamic market changes will gradually overtake and overwhelm the business.

Upgrading means adding one or more *profit centers* to an existing business, whereby the rate of potential return is far ahead of any resultant increase in operating costs.

In times past when a steam locomotive was on "dead center," no amount of steam pressure could move the train. In business, an organization which does not move with the changing times can quietly slip into dead center. One of the best-known retail organizations in the world, with almost limitless financial resources, quietly slipped into dead center by not moving with the changes in the consumer market. The formerly prosperous Robert Hall mercantile chain ascribed its recent dissolution to the fact that it didn't "upgrade."

Profits are a function of acute awareness. Upgrading should be a continuous process. It should cover every aspect of the business: the building structure, the products and services, and even the upgrading of management and customers. The total corporate image, the impression on the trade, markets, and consumers, should be dynamic and constantly upgraded. Recall that the largest domestic corporation evolved from the Standard Oil Company to Esso to Exxon. This dynamic image upgrading cost millions of dollars, but top management felt satisfied that it was money well spent.

Another example of effective upgrading is that of a large, variety-store chain. Originally, its stores were low-rent, small-inventory, mom-and-pop type, with a drab-looking image and doing a gross volume business of approximately $100,000 a year.

"Mom and pop" were fortunate if they netted $7000 after working long hours.

Then the chain undertook a wide-ranging program of upgrading. Now stores are located in prime locations in new shopping centers, sales space has been increased dramatically, and inventory substantially increased, with the results that the public image of the operation has improved greatly and gross sales per store average $700,000 per unit. It is clear that continuous upgrading is a substantial asset.

Upgrading Adds New Profit Dimensions

There are many additional examples of how upgrading is used today to add new profit dimensions to the business:

1. J. C. Penney has adopted a new upgrade image. Whereas the name was formerly associated with rural, minimally styled apparel, the new image—as conveyed in increased ad space—is that of high-quality, high-fashion, modern apparel for both men and women. Both image and appeal have been upgraded. Sales have resultingly escalated.

2. Korvettes department store in New York stresses "The Other Korvettes" in its television and other advertisements. The thrust is toward showing modern, up-to-date fashion as contrasted with ordinary, nonfashionable, discount store merchandise. Substantially increased sales and profits were ascribed to this new upgraded theme.

3. Even increasing prices can be considered upgrading. Ponderosa Steak Houses, for example, has increased its prices, as part of its upgrading program, without affecting patronage. Credit cards are also being considered.

4. Zum Zum restaurants, formerly Bavarian in theme, adopted what is termed "A New Accent," offering a greater diversification of menu specialties. Consequently, the average customer bill of approximately $1.50 has been increased to $2.50 or more.

5. Der Wiener Schnitzel has introduced its "Concept 90" program, which represents a completely upgraded structure and image.

6. A business called Hamburger Hamlet publicized its "$6,000 Baked Apple" as a means of conveying an upgraded image that puts it on a level above usual hamburger eating places.

9. SHARING ADVERTISING COSTS

Constant, repetitive advertising and trade-name impact are vital to today's marketing technique. Generally speaking, the business that has the greatest advertising exposure in a market is the business that will dominate that market.

This is particularly true of present-day electronic media, especially television. It's a medium that has powerful influence. It is all-pervasive in its impact, entering the living rooms of most homes in an area to sell products and services on, practically, a person-to-person basis. The single-unit operation (and even several units) cannot compete with this medium. An abundance of units in an area is required to "share" this expenditure to provide maximum coverage and *total market* utilization. Conversely, a serious, nonproductive expense is to have advertising coverage, by electronic media, that reaches areas not served by a company unit.

10. ADVANTAGES OF "CLUSTER" EXPANSION

A prerequisite of advertising saturation is "cluster" expansion. Cluster expansion is the establishment of multiple branches within a common, natural trading area, covered by a common, dominant medium. It is a form of saturation expansion, designed to restrict competition. One of the great advantages of this type operation is its ability to share the benefits and costs of advertising in the trading area. Here, television costs become reasonable—and affordable—when shared by clustered branches.

This type of advertising has achieved intensive market penetration for McDonald's, Burger King, Kentucky Fried Chicken, and others. It is noteworthy that, recently, McDonald's budgeted $81 million for advertising. How big is that? Think of some *25 billion* hamburgers already sold!

11. ADI MARKETING CONCEPT

ADI is trade "code" for "area dominant influence." This concept refers to the extent of advertising exposure required, in the dominant media of a particular market, to result in a traffic flow which produces a preselected level of sales.

The concept is also employed to determine the number of branches or sales units required, in a particular market, to produce that certain level of sales on an economic basis. For example, the metropolitan ADI of a fast-food hamburger chain may require as many as fifty (or more) separate units, supporting the prime-time television advertising on an economic basis, to accommodate the desired customer traffic.

Thus, ADI to be economically feasible requires clustered operations.

12. COPING WITH BUSINESS FLUCTUATIONS

Business declines, surges, and emerging market trends are circumstances which require responsive strategies and tactics. As an example, with one woman in five now in the labor force, fewer meals are prepared at home, resulting in an increase in restaurant dining. This trend has caused a reduced purchase of groceries, resulting in a decline in grocery and supermarket business, and a proliferation of fast-food restaurants, especially the family type where several persons can eat for less than $20, rather than the $50 cost of the white-tablecloth type of restaurant.

It is also stated that automobiles are currently run for 5 years, prior to replacement. It is assumed that this deferment of capital investment results from the economic pressures of currency inflation. It is yet to be demonstrated whether or not the long-term car owner will maintain the car with new mufflers, transmissions, and tuneups, thereby determining the growth trends of these specialized automotive services.

There is also the matter of the impact of ecology legislation to be considered—it will create new industries and modify old industry practices. In this labyrinth there will be great new business opportunities.

13. BRANCHISING WITHIN EXISTING BUSINESSES

Existing businesses seek to find experienced management to operate a secondary profit-center business in their behalf, either within their present building structure or within a separate site. This enables accelerated unit expansion and increased earnings potential. As examples:

1. Gas stations, since the oil scarcity, have actively sought to acquire new profit-center businesses to occupy available bays or, in some cases, the complete station. Such businesses include convenient food stores, donut shops, auto-parts sales centers, bicycle sales and service, tobacco shops, etc.

2. Burger King licenses existing businesses including Greyhound Bus (a multiple-unit licensee), Horn & Hardart (over twenty branch units), and Carroll's Hamburgers (over a hundred branch units).

3. H&R Block Co. participates with banks, department stores, etc., for its tax preparation services.

4. A business called Wine Cellars has department stores as licensees. A completely self-imaged structure is built within each department store.

14. OBTAINING GOOD SITES

Good sites are becoming scarcer. Construction costs have also escalated. Hence, many companies, instead of establishing new branch units in selected marketing areas, are now going the "acquisition route." The reasoning is that it costs less to acquire an existing company now operating in an eligible site than to build from scratch. Business starts are thus accelerated, and high construction costs are avoided.

There have recently been many examples of multiple-unit acquisitions. In addition, many franchised chains have been buying back their multiple-unit franchisees. Wendy's and Ponderosa are two recent examples. The Pizza Hut's 3000-unit network was acquired by Pepsi-Cola.

Branchising
Options

This chapter presents a wide variety of optional Branchising concepts.

The concepts provide the basic workable ideas, but their implementation requires supplementation of your own. It is up to each company to discover capabilities that have applicability to its own needs. In effect the ideas herein provide the blank spaces that enable you to fill in your own program objectives. To express it another way, these ideas present the raw clay; it's up to you to do the required shaping and molding to fit your needs.

It's possible to use a blend of several concepts in a sort of mix-and-match process or to modify, supplement, or add on to the ideas presented.

The various concepts are not theoretical. In most instances they have been used effectively by resourceful businesses.

Study of these plans often produces a ripple effect. Many new collateral ideas may flow forth.

FRANCHISING AS A BRANCHISING TECHNIQUE

One of the better-known Branchising techniques is "franchising." Franchising is only one of a large number of options available to a Branchising program.

What Is Franchising?

Franchising is a well-tested and proven method of accelerating market distribution, which results in (1) fees, royalties, and new market penetration for the sponsor and (2) security and growth for the entrepreneurs. The franchisor provides the managerial expertise and the franchisees provide the distributive effort.

The traditional vertical chain of command has now evolved into a horizontal managerial relationship. Practical business considerations are responsible for this change, to a marked degree, but franchise regulations now extant in fifteen states have also been influential.

 THREE

Status of Franchising

Franchising continues to break new records in sales, employment, and the number of establishments. Several factors have contributed to this phenomenal growth: New fields are being developed constantly for franchised operations, and foreign markets are being expanded. Also, franchisees are benefiting from the use of trade names, marketing expertise, acquisition of a distinctive business appearance, standardization of products and services, and advertising support by the parent organization.

Franchise sales of goods and services, according to a Department of Commerce study, were expected to reach $280 billion in 1978, an increase of 29 percent over sales reported for 1976, while the number of franchised establishments was around 468,000 in 1978, up from 443,263 in 1976. Employment in franchising, including part-time workers and working proprietors, was estimated at 3,792,341 in 1976, a gain of 8 percent from the 1975 level of 3,511,042 persons.

Successful Franchising

By merging local capital and energy with a national reputation, supervision, proven products, and the proven techniques of running such a business, an amalgamation is created whereby both parties are mutually interested in the success of the business. If local franchises are not successful, the manufacturer's program cannot succeed. If the manufacturer becomes lax or does not adapt to changing market conditions, the "system" of franchisees will falter. It is believed that this mutually dependent relationship is responsible for the fewer failures in franchising than in other forms of retailing. If true, this reduces waste in the economy.

When the elements required for success in franchising are discussed, it must be remembered that the term "franchising" refers only to a system (channel) of distribution. There are many factors other than the choice and utilization of a channel of distribution which ultimately determine a firm's success or failure, for example, product quality. If the product is unacceptable to the market for which it is intended, no channel of distribution will be able to deliver adequate sales. Also, other factors can be beyond the control of the firm. An enfranchised firm dependent, for example, upon the use of leased telephone lines to deliver its service cannot succeed if it is unable to secure access to any lines. Thus, when the determinants required for success in franchising are assessed, they must be considered from the "all other factors being equal" approach.

Hence, franchising is not effective, per se, but only when a certain set of conditions prevail.

The franchisee is a local, independent businessperson who establishes a reputation and identity with the franchisor which is much closer than that of the usual independent "middleman." The franchisee is willing to submerge some of his personal identity because there are advantages to be gleaned from the reputation and resources of a larger company.

Thus, it is observed that franchising is an arrangement whereby the franchisor, who has developed a successful product or service plus a successful pattern or formula for the conduct of the particular kind of business, extends franchisees the right or privilege of participating in that business as long as they follow the parent's established pattern or formula of operation.

Obligations of the Franchisor

In the usual franchise relationship, the franchisor provides the following to the franchisee:

- Use of the company trademark
- Store location analysis and counsel. Assistance in purchase of site or negotiation of building lease
- Assistance in the purchase of necessary initial equipment
- Store construction or remodeling plans
- Financial assistance in the form of a loan, allowing purchases on account, or countersigning loans obtained from a third party
- Training of management and employees
- Visit by a field representative during the first week or more of preopening, opening, and "grand opening"
- Program of national advertising, publicity, and public relations
- Preparation of materials for local advertising
- Merchandising assistance
- Record-keeping books and tax bulletins

Manual of operating procedures

On-the-spot field counseling on all aspects of conducting the business. Specialized home office counsel when required

Continual feedback of information on new developments

Savings through centralized purchasing

Newer Types of Franchising

During recent years, expansion of franchising has reached a variety of retail and service industries including fast-food restaurants, lodging, rentals, business aids, personal services, bicycle shops, lawn services, real estate, and wholesaling.

The growth sector of the restaurant industry continues to be the franchised food business. Fast-food restaurant sales reached almost $14 billion in 1976, about 13 percent over the previous year's level. There were an estimated 47,167 franchised food outlets, almost 4200 more than a year earlier.

Other significant growth sectors in nontraditional franchising include nonfood retailing; automotive products and services; construction, home improvements, and cleaning services; and convenience stores.

Franchised Retail Sales Growing

Retail sales of franchising firms—both independent and company-owned—reached an estimated $193 billion in 1976 and accounted for more than 90 percent of all nontraditional franchising gross receipts. In 1977, retail franchising rose to almost 13 percent and amounted to nearly $218 billion. The trend toward multiunit own-

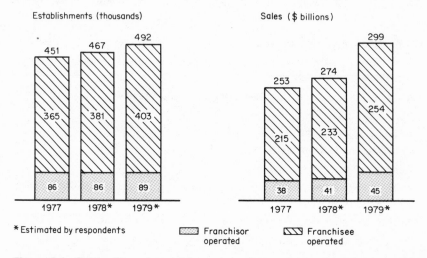

Figure 3-1 Total sales and establishments.

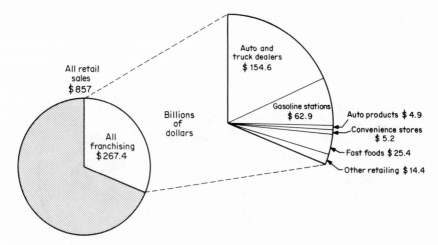

Figure 3-2 Franchising encompassed 31 percent of retail sales in 1979.

ership by franchisees—especially in the fast-food sector—continues strong, and franchisors are increasingly granting rights to develop large regional markets.

TRAINING AS A BRANCHISING CONCEPT

What is the "training" profit potential of your business? If your business requires even elementary technical knowledge, you are in a position to charge a fee to train potential personnel for your industry. The travel industry and real estate sales are two prime examples of areas requiring some technical knowledge.

Not only can a company charge a reasonable fee for such schooling, but it is in a position to benefit from a viable ongoing association and from this controlled labor pool created by its training school. For example, H&R Block runs a tax-training school charging an initial tuition fee. Thus, thousands of trained personnel provide the company with an inventory of skilled workers, not carried as overhead but available to offset peak demand periods for H&R Block franchisees.

Also, this training concept has the potential residual benefit of creating a market for its own products and services.

As an example, one company in the manufacture of men's toiletries offers a most professional hair-styling seminar every 6 months around the country and charges just a nominal fee for attendance and training. Attendance is normally quite large, and the participants are encouraged, through a feeling of obligation to the parent company, to stock and constantly reorder the company's manufactured items.

PROFIT FROM YOUR TRADEMARK

Your trademark, patent, and other techniques constitute valuable potential assets that may be salable or rentable to individuals or businesses, both nationally and internationally. They may constitute latent, unrecognized profit centers.

For example, Century 21 grants the use of its trademark to realtors; Nathan's (famed turn-of-the-century hot dog emporium) offers to rent its name to those seeking a nostalgic tie-in with their products or services.

Another organization, called Dairy King, grants the use of its name to previously unaffiliated ice-cream parlors and related food businesses. Thus the single-unit business is given the opportunity to join a network of related businesses and to achieve economies and other advantages of scale.

These examples all add up to the fact that your name can constitute a valuable asset. Utilize it as such.

Royalty and Licensing Agreements. These agreements, linked to trademarks and patents, have as their objective the creation of residual income, plus a degree of quality control. The trademark is protected through federal registration. However, it may take a year or longer to obtain this protection. Many states will register a trademark and somewhat more quickly than the federal government. Also, unregistered trademarks enjoy some protection under the common law.

To retain rights to a trademark, an owner must maintain enough control over the licensees to assure that they adhere to the quality standards for which the trademark stands. Also, the impact of the Sherman Antitrust laws must be considered in relation to trademark licensing and possible restraint of trade.

SYSTEMS CENTERS AND NETWORK BRANCHISING

To understand network Branchising, view it as a giant spider's web. At the center of the web is the "systems center." The various strands that radiate outward constitute separate but related businesses that utilize a common trademark, and, furthermore, new "strands" can always be added, creating additional profit centers. For example, Figure 3-3 indicates the network of businesses related to bridal services that are all administered from a single systems center.

As the various related businesses proliferate, additional systems centers can be added to service each of these networks.

In the field of network Branchising, these component factors are prerequisites:

- A well-known respected name or trademark
- An adequate table of organization
- Sophisticated management
- A viable program format or "system"

The "Atomic" Trademark

We have had occasion to observe the applicability of this Branchising network concept while in Germany: My host proudly showed me that the suit he wore was labeled "Atomic," his tie and shoes were Atomic, and his wristwatch was Atomic. His wife showed that their TV was Atomic, as well as their freezer and dishwasher. And the tickets they ordered for the theater that evening came from a place called Atomic.

In this instance, Atomic applied to "better living" products and services, offering items from appliances to clothes to entertainment.

Atomic comprised, within its fold, existing businesses in each of these fields that have been redesigned to conform to the Atomic image and format. It also included new, start-up businesses, all accepted under the Atomic trade name and mark. An establishment fee and a continuing management, or program supporting, fee is charged.

The benefits of network Branchising are apparent. It achieves high-yield management, volume economies, management efficiencies, and advertising saturation at "shared" minimum cost.

PARTNERSHIPS AS BRANCHISED PROFIT CENTERS

A partnership is a contract between two or more competent persons to join together in business, to share the profits in accordance with the partnership agreement, and to assume unlimited liability for the affairs of the firm.

There are many ways in which the partnership concept can be applied: The Branchisor can be a general partner and the Branchisee, the limited partner, and vice

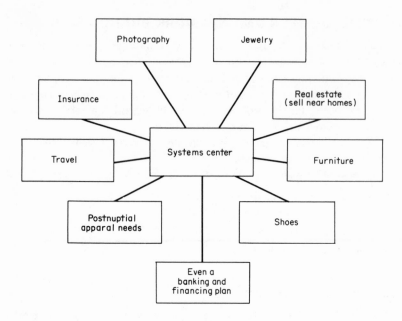

Figure 3-3 Branching of related businesses, e.g., bridal services, through trademark utilization.

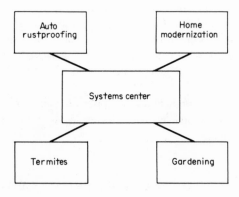

Figure 3-4 Internal Branching, e.g., a department store, functioning as a systems center.

versa (see below). Operating as a general partner it is also possible to appoint local operating managers who, in effect, become associated general partners.

General Partnership

A general partnership is an association of two or more individuals to operate a business for profit as co-owners. The major advantage is that double taxation is avoided, as there is no company income tax. The tax levy is paid by the individual partners.

The danger of this form of business organization is that each partner is fully liable, personally, for the debts of the partnership. This aspect of unlimited personal liability for a partnership often militates against its use.

Limited Partnership

A limited partnership has the benefits of a general partnership but avoids the danger of unlimited liability for all partners. It is organized so that one of the partners has unlimited liability, just like a general partnership. However, the limited partner's liability is limited to only the amount invested in the partnership; the limited partner has no personal liability beyond his original investment. The limited partner may not participate in management and may not contribute services to the firm. The limited partner risks the loss of limited liability if he violates these provisions. The possible application of the limited partnership concept to Branchising is to establish the parent company as the general partner and the absentee investors as the limited partner. Full liability is restricted to the *general partner* or *partners*. Usually, one of the general partners is appointed operating manager on a salaried basis. To limit liability for the general partners they may form a corporation.

The individual general partners can also be limited partners, as well.

In one such arrangement, a management fee of 15 percent was assessed and a percent of profits was also part of the consideration. In addition, the general partner could have the right to buy limited partner shares or additional shares at some stated figure.

BUSINESS-WITHIN-A-BUSINESS CONCEPT

Branchising may also be achieved by employing the business-within-a-business concept. Basically, this is another technique for the more intensive use of capital. It consists of adding one or more potential profit centers of allied businesses to an existing operation, while increasing operating costs only moderately. The effect would be a magnified net income. It amounts to "leveraging" profits by more intensive asset use at only a moderate increase in operating costs. Some examples will illustrate the technique:

Certain automobile service stations, desiring to exploit traffic flow more intensively, have closed a number of work bays and have substituted other businesses in the space, e.g., convenient food items, donut shops, tobacco stores, etc.

Surprisingly but, perhaps, logically (in view of the inroads of family-type restaurants into grocery shopping), many supermarkets are opening full-service restaurants, some with their own entrances and exits.

Department stores may be the equivalent of Branchises, paying establishment fees and royalties, and seeking viable profit-center businesses. Their management expertise now includes various complete store units under the same roof. One such is Wine Cellars, a completely separate chain of wine stores located within department stores.

These are not small, tentative thrusts into new areas. Some are very large. For example, Rockwood Industries lease men's and boys' apparel departments in Woolco stores with an annual volume in excess of $24 million.

H&R Block, specialists in income tax preparation, have in excess of 3000 tax centers throughout the country, with hundreds of units located in local banks and department stores, including the mail-order retail outlets of Sears, Roebuck and Montgomery Ward.

Another development is, for example, a "common roof," housing several separate, unrelated businesses, having in common only the mutually stimulated traffic. One particular unit is known as the Merchant of Venice and is located in California. It houses four separate businesses under one roof: (1) an antique shop, (2) a cabinet shop, (3) a refinishing service, and (4) a prosperous restaurant. Surprisingly, everything in the restaurant is for sale, including the wine racks, the furniture, the tableware, and even the plants.

EXPANDING THROUGH DEALERSHIPS

A dealership constitutes a sales entity that undertakes to sell a line of products (usually a well-known brand name) for a manufacturer or wholesaler.

To obtain the dealership, a commitment is made to purchase an initial inventory and to meet a minimum sales quota. In some instances, a commitment is made to do a minimum amount of local advertising.

Operating at their own expense, dealerships can prove an effective sales force. The dealership agreement usually continues as long as the dealer meets prescribed sales quotas.

The parent company assures the dealer of product availability, maintains quality control, conducts advertising and sales promotions, and provides training and management assistance.

Dealerships can provide rapid and extensive market penetration to a company with minimal capital outlay. Each dealership constitutes a potential profit center.

ESTABLISHING A BUYING SERVICE

A typical buying service, which acts as the buyer for a group and obtains economies of size, is a conventional operation. It is generally organized on an establishment-fee basis, plus a continuing monthly fee. In certain instances the service may also obtain a designated percentage of the purchase price of certain commitments.

The usual buying service not only assists members in making purchases at volume-discount prices, but offers other assistance, such as advising on management problems and arranging cooperative advertising among its members. Some services will even advise members on site selection for new units; assist in obtaining financing; advise on store design, construction, and personnel training; and may provide computerized central accounting services.

Examples of buying-service-type networks include the International Grocers Association (IGA) in the grocery field, Buy-Rite in the liquor field, and True Value and Ace Hardware in the hardware field.

Some of these services have 2000 or more units. At wholesale levels, computerized techniques in distribution and warehousing provide faster and more efficient service. Also, private-label lines add to the profit potential.

There are literally hundreds of buying-service types of businesses serving a great diversification of trades. They help the small business to narrow differences with the larger chains and to compete effectively. Their services include assistance with the following aspects:

Product selection	Store signs
Business management	Improvement of store image
Advertising and promotions	Inventory control
Proper record-keeping	Avoidance of pilferage
Personnel recruitment and training	

ADVISORY SERVICES BY MANAGEMENT CONSULTANTS

Professional management consultants offer their expertise to companies in varied businesses. Compensation is on a designated per hour or retainer basis, plus (in some instances) a percentage of the increase in sale or profits resulting from their efforts. Thus, each of the consultative clients serviced by the management consultant constitutes a separate "profit center." This profitability concept is projectable on a nationwide basis.

To project this principle to the Branchising concept, you may consider the establishment of a network of clients on a management consultant basis, thus, in effect, selling your "continuing advice" for a designated fee as spelled out by contractual provisions.

Possible management consultant fees constitute an initial fee for the program installation followed by an agreed-on retainer fee. Each of these management consultant arrangements constitutes another potential profit center.

In such an operation, the parent becomes an advisor or "management consultant" to the operator and supplies him with the expert knowledge and skills required for the successful operation of the business on a continuing basis. For these services the parent, just as consultants in other fields, receives an initial "establishment fee" and a continuing retainer fee for management consulting.

Such a contractual arrangement is often characteristic of motels. Another example is that of a boat-restaurant which cruises the shorelines. In this instance the operations manager, functioning as general partner, represents the investor group; the investors are the limited partners.

Used in Branchising, the concept of management consulting borrows from the techniques of the old public utility holding companies. In those complexes, specialized services were restricted to and performed by management advisory companies on an internal-fee basis.

In Branchising, the Branchisor could act as the "network advisor" or could organize a wholly owned subsidiary to function as the network advisor. In either case, the Branchisees would pay a fee for services rendered.

Management Contract

Another Branchising concept is the "management contract," commonly found in real estate transactions and hotel management.

By this method, the Branchisor sells its operational expertise, name, and image without risks of ownership to an investor/developer.

The Branchisor assumes complete operational responsibility and receives a fee based on a percent of the gross revenue plus an incentive computed on a share of the profits.

The Branchisee assumes a passive position when it comes to day-to-day management but is financially responsible for the business. The Branchisee thus retains a team offering a wide range of professional management talent, proven methods of operation, and accumulated experience. He probably would have additional advantages of the operational company's talent in recruiting help, marketing and sales assistance, buying power, and borrowing funds.

The management contract for the Branchisor is a low-cost method of expansion without affecting the balance sheet and without any liability for bearing losses.

CONDOMINIUM CONCEPT

Is your type of business divisible into segments? It may be possible to sell the whole operation more quickly by dividing it into components and selling it piece by piece.

Condominiums, generally, sell their assets to subscribers, who become owners of a particular physical asset. The peripheral services usually remain as the property of the Branchisor who for an appropriate continuing fee operates them for the benefit of the condominium owners.

For example, a well-known campground sold its parking facilities as a condominium but retained its supplemental facilities, such as the swimming pool and food services. The management also receives a fee for renting the unoccupied spaces as agent for the owners.

This method lends itself to facilitating financing. As an example, a racquet ball emporium having forty courts was "sold" as separate playing courts, and each was offered for $50,000 (a total of $200,000).

Managers of condominium complexes operate on the basis of a long-term relationship between the buyer and the managers. After the initial sale, upon which the management obtains a profit, the maintenance and support services are provided by management on a continuous revenue basis.

This concept has also been applied in the medical and other fields by means of offering a centralized laboratory, library, computerized billing, and other services.

Cooperatives

The primary difference between a condominium and a cooperative is that, in the first case, the participant owns his own apartment or unit. This concept of "property" ownership enables the participant to mortgage his own property.

In a cooperative venture, the participant is a stockholder having an equity in the entire project. The only alternative the stockholder has is to borrow on the shares or to sell the shares. Usually it is very difficult to borrow on the stock by using the stock as collateral because there is no market for the shares and, therefore, no accurate method for valuing them.

Should the participant desire to sell his shares, there are usually covenants requiring that the new tenant be suitable and desirable to the remaining tenants.

Wide Applicability of Condominiums

The condominium concept also has valid applications in areas other than real estate. For example, a large chain of variety or department stores could sell the components or "departments" of the operation. Such an approach might be applied in the automotive field. One large facility could be divided into the following sections: (1) air conditioning, (2) radio and CB, (3) brakes, shocks, springs, front-end, (4) mufflers, (5) engine exchange, (6) transmission, (7) body work and painting, (8) auto glass shop, and (9) upholstery repairs.

It is quickly apparent that a number of these "sections," such as mufflers, transmissions, and body work and painting, already have been promoted into nationwide "specialist" chains. What has not been attempted, to date, is the creation of an all-inclusive operation consisting of all these sections. This could be accomplished by selling each section, with the parent company operating and managing the total facility.

Again, the same concept could be applied to the home repair and remodeling industry. The major facility would include carpenters, cabinet makers, electricians, painters, roofers, glaziers, plumbers, masons, flooring, and air conditioning.

Here, the parent company, in addition to providing and managing the facility, would provide the answering service, typing, record-keeping, advertising, and promotion.

The basic concept could be applicable to a wide variety of both production and service industries, such as the previously mentioned medical field, in graphic arts, and perhaps in law, where the operator would provide the law library, secretarial services, receptionist, and switchboard.

DIRECT SALES

Achieve representation of hundreds—even thousands—of salespersons selling your products. Virtually instant expansion.

Direct sales are made by commission merchants, independent businesspeople, selling on a straight commission basis. There are an estimated 200,000 such self-motivated persons operating in the direct sales industry. They are not carried on the payroll of the Branchisor, nor do they receive any "fringe" benefits. Achieving ongoing sales and earnings, they constitute profit centers.

Using such personnel for selling can result in the lowest cost of all distribution methods. Company overhead is low. The company has no financial obligation toward such direct sales agents until they make a sale of the company's product. Thereafter, a commission is due upon delivery of the goods and services.

Potential Income Source. Profits are on the goods sold less minimal distribution costs. There is no burden on working capital. In net effect, the sales agent makes a capital contribution to the company until his cost is recouped by a sales commission.

Some very excellent companies have availed themselves of this labor pool with

outstanding success, for example, Avon Products, the Electrolux Company, and the Fuller Brush Company. There are 200,000 direct sales agents available. Can they be recruited?

Use the trade publications *Salesman's Opportunity* and *Specialty Salesman.* The dedicated readership of these publications is staggering. Should you expect about twenty replies from a typical recruitment advertisement in *The Wall Street Journal,* you will be amazed to receive as many as two hundred (and possibly more) replies from a comparable advertisement in a direct sales magazine.

This experience demonstrates the self-motivation and aggressiveness of this type of salesperson. This "push" places these representatives inside of the prospects' homes, where products are personally demonstrated. It is this element in the sales effort which produces the results. For example, there was a company in the water-conditioning equipment industry whose product sold for $375. The same product was available at the local Sears, Roebuck store at a price of $125, yet the salesperson outsold Sears three-to-one. Why? It's the power of home demonstration.

Exceptional experience? Not at all. There is a shoe company with 20,000 direct salespeople on its staff. The average annual volume per salesperson is $500. That's $10 million in annual sales volume at *no* overhead cost.

LEASING CONCEPT

Leasing covers a wide spectrum of "rental" approaches including machinery, equipment, land, building, or an entire business enterprise.

In effect, this concept can provide various sources of multiple residual income for the Branchisor. The title to the property resides with the Branchisor, and the rental is income to the Branchisor and a deductible operating expense to the Branchisee. Continued revenue is obtained through the renting or the leasing of building, plant, equipment, or other tangible items. The basis of the relationship can be defined in the lease agreement. It can be combined with the licensing of trademarks and patents to give the parent company strong control over branch operations.

The rental of equipment can constitute individual profit centers. For example, one enterprising company pioneered in the rental of televisions to hotels, taverns, etc., and had literally thousands of profit centers paying so much per month, adding up to substantial ongoing profits. A franchising organization in the carpet-cleaning field "rents" its equipment to its 2000 franchisees. A foremost producer of machinery for the shoe industry leases its equipment. The telephone company, as another example, leases its extension phones at so much per month.

DEALER RENTAL PLANS

Leasing is also a means of obtaining dealers, by helping to finance the dealers and their customers, and thus achieving accelerated growth. The renting method of selling achieves quicker sales, ongoing utilization, and continuing income.

Under this plan, the branch dealer rents company products to the ultimate consumer. The company supplies the dealer with an initial rental inventory, intended for rental use and not for resale. The dealer then solicits leases and is responsible for each installation in his territory. For example, the dealer could collect the first and last month's rental at the time of installation. Thereafter, the company collects the rental.

For each lease the dealer sells, he receives a commission from the company, calculated on the monies collected over the life of the lease. As consideration for the territorial concession, the dealer provides labor and services for the units in his territory and the company provides all repair parts, free of charge. The company and the dealer agree upon a quota for the territory, and if it is not met, the agreement is canceled.

Under this plan the company has the advantage of an aggressive sales force at no overhead cost. The sales are paid for as the customer remits the rentals. On the other hand, the company must finance the entire inventory and carry the cost of the installations until they are written off under the lease agreements. For this purpose, the company must be adequately financed.

AREA CONTROLLERSHIPS

You can appoint regional distributors and decentralize your operation and commitments.

An area controller is a person or persons committed to the operation of the multiple units of a Branchise within a designated area. He is, in effect, a sub-Branchisor having "wholesale" control over multiple units.

Generally, the area controller's units are clustered together, thus achieving various economies of scale particularly in administration, advertising, and promotion. Usually they are located in an ADI area for coparticipated advertising economies; as many as twenty units or more may be included under their control.

The area controller can own and operate the units by himself, or can recruit the equivalent of local or satellite Branchisees to operate such units.

Generally, the area controller is a successful businessperson (on an executive level), well-financed, and able to withstand unforeseen financial problems in the development of a business. He is also a good manager.

In one case we are acquainted with, the area controller receives 50 percent of fees and royalties of those operations under his control.

The benefit of an area controller to the Branchisor is this: In today's economy it can prove too expensive to implement a Branchising program on a one-on-one basis. It is more efficient to deal with one person who has the responsibilities for multiple units.

In the franchising field, one prominent restaurant chain has twenty-four area controllers running 920 stores and doing an annual business in excess of a half-billion dollars.

There are many examples of the controllership concept in the food field, where the need for clustering has been recognized:

Arthur Treacher has espoused, constantly, the controllership concept in its licensing program.

Wendy's hamburgers has appointed controllers on a local, citywide, statewide, and even countrywide level.

Der Wiener Schnitzel had recently appointed an area controller (a Los Angeles meat firm) that plans to develop ten units in Oregon and Washington. They comment: "Controllerships are the key to future growth. It is difficult to grow one unit at a time."

Some individual, multiple-unit licensees of Burger King have as many as a hundred units.

Pizza Hut licensees operate as many as eighty units in some instances.

WHOLESALER AND RETAILER ASSOCIATIONS

Wholesaler and retailer associations act to obtain economies of size, share of advertising burdens, and provide mutual, managerial advice.

Cooperative- and wholesaler-sponsored groups are becoming increasingly important and diversified. IGA (in the retail grocery field), Buy Rite (in the liquor field), and Super Value (in hardware) are examples of cooperatives that have grown in recent years.

There are two broad types of wholesaler and retailer associations: voluntary chains and cooperative chains.

The "voluntary chain" is, fundamentally, a voluntary "membership" participation, usually offered by a wholesaler on behalf of stores within a related field. The wholesaler controls this operation and provides services on a businesslike, profit making basis.

The "cooperative chain" is formed by participating retailers. It is their child and their collective ownership, conceived to provide purchasing, promotional, and administrative benefits not normally available to the individual, nonaffiliated store.

Each of these concepts has grown greatly in recent years, as explained on the following pages.

Voluntary Chains

Wetterau Foods is one example of a highly successful wholesaler which vends its wares to a select group of retailers. Although they are independent operators, participating store owners have a close relationship with a single jobber and typically receive (for a fee) many additional services such as accounting, site selection, financing, training, and advertising. Computerized techniques in distribution and warehousing are providing greater efficiency. Private-label lines also help to increase profits.

Food and other merchandise are sold to affiliated retailers on a cost-plus basis, for example, 2 to 3½ percent, depending on delivery distance.

The network of Ben Franklin stores commenced as a voluntary cooperative that has evolved into a franchising chain comprising 2000-plus franchisees. Effective management guidance, promotions, and rapidity of service are some of the benefits offered to its affiliated franchisees.

Wholesaler and Retailer Chains

Wholesaler and retailer programs are of two types:

Individual Store Promotions.   The wholesaler assists a store in conducting one or a series of store sales featuring the wholesaler's product line.

Wholesaler-Sponsored Groups of Retailers.   The retailers participate under a common name or symbol. The wholesaler conducts an advertising and promotional campaign for the entire group and, also, may provide other services, such as computerized accounting, either free or at a reasonable price.

The members of this group usually promote the same item in the same advertisements, at the same sale price, and at the same time. The retailer benefits through the effective use of the advertising budget, by the advantage of promotional buying by the wholesaler, and through the collection and administration of "co-op" advertising funds from the manufacturer. Each retailer usually contributes a specific amount, weekly, to an advertising fund.

JOINT VENTURES

The joint venture, originating in antiquity when it was used to organize shipping ventures, is one of the oldest forms of business. It is generally created for one specific piece of business and is terminated when the business is concluded. Participation is in relation to a prescribed interest, and the business is conducted by a designated operations manager. Profits or losses are apportioned when this syndicate is dissolved. A joint venture can almost be regarded as a form of "temporary" partnership, unusual in the respect that it can be entered into by a corporation.

While joint venture agreements will vary substantially according to the practices of the industry in which the agreement is operative, certain elements are common to all syndicate agreements:

Date, name, and address of each syndicate party

Purpose of the joint venture

Amount of contribution by each syndicate member

Payment of amount contributed

Acquisition of property

Manner of holding title

Management of venture

Compensation of syndicate manager

Manager's indemnification

Liability of manager

Liability of participants

Division of profits

Payment of expenses

Payment of losses

Term of venture agreement

Arbitration of disputes

Interest payment on funds advanced

Deposit of funds

Default in payment of amount subscribed

Substitution of manager

Binding effect of manager's acts

Manner of giving notice

Subscribers not partners or agents

Binding effect of agreement

Leasing of business property

Termination or dissolution

Withdrawal of subscriber

Liquidation of business

Transfer of interest

A company can expand by establishing one or a network of joint venture arrangements in which each party makes precommitments relative to functions and ownership participation.

Joint venture arrangements vary greatly. Interests can be a majority type or a minority type. There can also be options to purchase increased equity interest based on predesignated performance.

A novel joint venture in the fast-foods field is an apt illustration. In this case the Branchisee was a corporation investing the money, and the parent company, the other corporation, investing expertise. Both of them owned 50 percent of the new joint venture corporation.

The Branchisee investing the money would get a reasonable return on its investment from the joint venture corporation, and both parties after two years would decide whether or not to continue the association based on certain criteria and options. If successful, sooner or later, one of the parties can exercise its options to buy out the other.

A SPECIAL JOINT VENTURE PLAN

Description of Plan

In this instance, a joint venture is arranged between a company and an individual (not corporation or partnership) for which there is no fee investment or royalty paid. A security deposit is obtained for use of inventory, fixtures, and equipment.

The company owns everything; it usually leases a storefront and makes, or buys for resale, the products sold. Often, the store was run previously by the parent company.

Purpose of Plan

This arrangement is used when the required capital investment, together with the necessary advertising budget, to build the store's sales volume would be greater than what most individuals would be prepared to meet.

Operating expenses are extremely low as compared to the previous arrangements, but the inventory investment is substantial. This business requires a large stock of items on hand, ordinarily beyond the means of licensees, to meet competition. Also, much financing is done on products sold. To a great extent, the profit of the parent company is made on the sale of the product. Sales ability, promotional techniques, and "specials" are a necessary part of this type of business and require close coordination with the parent company.

Arrangement of Plan

The security deposit represents 50 percent of the value of the inventory and fixtures, and it is adjusted periodically to reflect the actual physical inventory.

The following formula is used to determine the "gross profits" accruing to the participants: sales *minus* returns and allowances *minus* cost of goods sold *equal* gross profit. Subtract from this figure repairs, advertising costs, accounts receivable, and charge plan costs to obtain an "adjusted gross profit." This amount is split 50/50. The parent company pays monthly rent, bookkeeping, taxes, and insurance charges. The individual partner pays labor, utilities, employee taxes, upkeep and maintenance on the store, seasonal store decoration, supplies, bad debt expense, and other operating expenses.

Ramifications of Plan

The store must maintain an average gross profit that is satisfactory, relative to the experience of other stores. If it does not, the loss to the parent company is made up by (1) payment from the partner or (2) withdrawal of money out of the security deposit.

The parent company has great control over its partner by the ability to terminate the contract, with a 3-month notice, for many reasons, one of them being "uncooperativeness" of the partner. The partner does not have the same ease of termination.

REAL ESTATE CONTROL

Real estate control is the leasing and subleasing of property as a means of producing income and is frequently used by the major fast-food chains. Their use of this method merely supplements their normal franchise operations. Here, leasing and subleasing can be employed as a major tool of control and a source of volume-based residual income. It can be readily combined with trademarks and patent licensing to avoid normal franchising methods.

As an alternative or in addition to the license agreement, it may be possible to use a sublease arrangement with a volume-based override to provide residual income and reasonable control.

Today it is not uncommon in real estate transactions for the developer to insist upon a minimum guarantee of a 12 percent return on land and buildings (occasionally 12 percent on buildings and 10 percent on land) against a percentage rent of 6 percent of gross sales, whichever is higher. (Six percent is most common, but it can vary from 4 to 8.5 percent.)

PARTY PLAN CONCEPT

Have your products and services actively displayed and sold in homes, by homemakers, in any locality throughout the country. This is known as the "party plan."

Become part of a billion-dollar enterprise!

Party plans are particularly popular during recessionary or inflationary periods when most households need to supplement income—even within the so-called "affluent" neighborhoods—in order to cope with recurring "money pressures."

The mechanics of a party plan are as follows:

Homemakers are recruited to serve as hostess for a "party" and then invite relatives, friends, and acquaintances. During the course of this friendly party, your products are demonstrated in a relaxed atmosphere, over tea and cake. The demonstration is made to a congenial, receptive audience, who attend the party with an awareness that they will be asked to purchase something. Thus they are responsive to an effective sales effort. Consequently, substantial sales are often achieved.

As one example, in a city of 250,000 people, an average of 125 "parties" were held per week with an average sale of $150 per party. Usually it is all cash "on the spot." At each party, one or more hostesses are recruited for future parties. Representatives are given incentives to recruit more representatives and can advance to managerial status over a group.

SELLING SHARES

Existing Corporation Concept

Where the principal shareholder of a corporation owns 100 percent of the voting shares, the public sale of 49 percent would not affect absolute control of the corporation. Applied in the Branchising concept, the branch operator or manager would be among the minority shareholders of the operation. In order that the branch operator may participate fairly in profits without jeopardizing the control of the parent company, the branch operator's stock interest could consist of a combination of voting and nonvoting shares that have equal participation in earnings.

Going Business Concept

The principal stockholder of a private company sells a minority interest in the corporation (up to 49 percent) to Branchisees. The basis of the relationship is specified in the corporate bylaws.

When a corporation is privately owned, the major stockholder may sell up to 49 percent without losing absolute control of the corporation. Prior to the sale of any shares, an attorney should be consulted so that the principal stockholder avoids the illegality of distributing unregistered stock.

There are a variety of ways of using corporate stock as an incentive for management, for example, stock option plans and retirement plans, such as the ESOP and the ESOT (see page 80). Also, a combination of classes of shares may be employed in order to give Branchisees a profit sharing incentive, while maintaining absolute control of the Branchisor corporation.

In some instances, particularly those of younger persons who can't afford to meet the required investment, the Branchisee will invest in as little as 10 percent of the stock and be given an option to acquire a larger interest out of his current earnings.

Another alternative to financing is to organize each unit as a corporation with the parent company being the minority stockholder. It may be possible, also, to put all the stock in a "voting trust" in favor of the parent company, thereby giving the parent company voting control during the formative period.

CATALOG CORNERS

Catalogs provide an opportunity to establish dozens, hundreds, perhaps even thousands of sales outlets—at minimal expense.

The technique operates as follows: In each community, stores having a good traffic flow, such as drugstores, department stores, and general stores, are recruited to establish a "catalog corner." Such a "corner" comprises a table and a chair, a copy of your catalog (affixed by a chain and lock to the table), plus a supply of order forms. Customers use this catalog corner to scan the pages of the catalog and to prepare their orders, which are given to the store proprietor for transmittal.

The store proprietor benefits in various ways: The catalog corner brings added traffic flow into the store and it constitutes an added profit center since it generates additional income. The catalog, in effect, increases the store's salable inventory without increased investment. Hence, the store now doing $200,000 a year in sales can increase its volume to $300,000 a year—or more—without increasing physical inventory.

The Branchisor benefits because of the acquisition of literally thousands of sales outlets at little expense.

INDEPENDENT SALES REPRESENTATIVES

This representative is an independent salesperson, who may sell a number of different lines of merchandise. He is the official representative of companies in specified territories and has his own clientele, with whom he is in contact continuously. He is also known as a "commission merchant." His remuneration varies from company to company: He may work on a salary plus bonus (drawing account against commissions) or on a straight commission, with the latter being the most common.

In most cases, the independent sales representatives pay all of their own expenses and the company incurs no costs until the merchandise is sold. Commissions paid range from a low of 3 percent to a high of 25 percent. Commission rates tend to vary with the industry and its profit structure.

The method of distributing products by independent sales representatives has attractive features. No overhead sales staff cost and no cost until a product is sold, and then, in effect, the buyer pays the sales commission, which is built into the price. However, the results are uneven: success for one company and abject failure for another. Why?

It is axiomatic that most independent representatives carry several lines. Unless they can make money with a line, no loyalty is developed.

Success with independent sales representatives requires that the company provide at least as much support for them as it does for salaried salespeople. This means a lead development program, product information, sales meetings, good literature, competitive pricing, good deliveries, and an attractive commission paid honestly and promptly.

Working with independent sales representatives requires sales experience plus the temperament to manage and motivate individuals who are not employees and who are not being paid for their efforts until successful.

There are sales specialists in product categories, as well as those who specialize in selling a variety of products to specific customer categories. Talents and education range from degreed engineers, handling highly technical products, to relatively unsuccessful plodders.

There are certain principles to observe should you intend to use independent sales representatives:

1. Study recruitment methods to ascertain you are attracting the best salespeople for your products and prospective customers.

2. Hire a sales manager who either has successful experience working with independent sales representatives or has the capacity and willingness to learn how.

3. Provide the salespeople with good literature, easy-to-understand specification sheets, clear price lists, and product samples when feasible and advantageous.

VENDING AND RACK JOBBING

Vending

Create a vending division for your company: Build custom machines, place them on locations, and service them by company staff.

Operate your company-owned vending division in conjunction with local independent operators. The usual way to get independent operators is to sell them a certain minimum number of machines with an initial inventory and guaranteed locations.

Bear in mind that a successful vending operation depends on the traffic density at the machine locations, and profitability, therefore, depends upon resupplying operators with your product rather than depending upon the sale of more "deals."

Rack Jobbing

Rack jobbing is a type of nonmechanical vending. The capital investment for equipment is nominal, and product sales tend to be a function of traffic. Space rental may be keyed to the area occupied or a nominal percentage of gross sales. Your own staff can replenish the racks, or this task may be contracted to a jobber, leaving your responsibility to only the manufacture of the product and the supply of the vending racks. The distribution and sale of the product are done by the jobber.

Merchandise of a particular class does well with this method, such as greeting cards, women's stockings, health products, food spices, and a myriad of small-sized products.

The parent company may sell the racks to licensees who will place them, purchase your product, and restock. This is a distribution system that is both low-cost and effective.

LICENSING EXISTING BUSINESSES

There is a great potential in the Branchising of related existing businesses. Consider this rationale:

The very concept of Branchising requires a sophisticated data systems center. This systems center can help to make profitable many types of businesses or can expand the potential of existing businesses.

For example, one company in the auto-body conditioning field reconverted existing, archaic, auto-body shops and sold these remodeled shops as "turnkey operations" to waiting groups of investors.

In the real estate field, realtors operate under the name of Century 21 or the Red Carpet. Another organization licensed confectionary stores under the name of Dairy King, thus capitalizing on the many thousands of nonaffiliated small confectionary stores.

SALE OF PARTIAL PROFITS

Here is another interesting and attractive Branchising technique: Instead of selling your business, or part of it, arrange to sell part of *your profits* only. You can keep everything above that sum. For example, sell a realizable income of $25,000. If the business earns more, e.g., $50,000 or $75,000, you merely retain the balance.

This is a simple concept but its very simplicity makes it effective. The relationship between you and your Branchisee is clear and easily monitored.

Hence, as Branchisor you can, in effect, establish hundreds, and even thousands, of units and establish earnings records, and, thereupon, sell participations in future profits.

This plan may be considered a security and should be reviewed by your legal counsel prior to go-ahead.

A technique used by a retail chain of clothing stores was as follows: On each new unit, the Branchisor would sell 20 percent of the potential profit but retain 80 percent of it to consolidate earnings with the parent company. An investor would buy the percentage for $50,000 guaranteeing him a 15 percent return on his money each year ($7,500) or 20 percent of the profits, whichever was greater. The $50,000 represented about half of the total investment needed.

The Branchisee has the right to redeem his investment at the rate of 20 percent a year after the first year. The Branchisor has the same rights, if the Branchisee does not use his right to redeem the Branchisee's 20 percent in full or part after the fifth year.

Movie studios also have espoused a system of "splitting profits," and some authors —including the author of *The Exorcist*—have earned millions of dollars through this arrangement.

BUSINESS POSITIONING

Does your business conform to the times? Or is it backdated 10 years and more, so that it may not constitute a competitive factor in today's market?

To succeed, a business must be "positioned." That is, it should have a distinctiveness permitting it to penetrate an established market with a product or service not supplied by other vendors.

As one illustration, Wendy's hamburgers became spectacularly successful in a short period of time because it positioned itself to provide "fresh, juicy" hamburgers as contrasted with the pre-frozen hamburgers of its competitors. Thus, instead of competing with the "giants" in their field, on an equated basis, Wendy's filled a marketing niche that they discerned was unfilled at the time. They also added a drive-in service window, something not available by competitors. Thus through positioning they were able to use a *competitive omission* to maneuver themselves into almost instant popularity.

Nat Sherman, a tobacconist, positioned himself among the tobacco giants by evaluating what they did and doing something *different*. His cigarettes were imprinted in a rainbow of colors to fit all apparel and occasions, and were longer and had unusual tips. His cigars were flatter, leaner, twisted, and otherwise different. These differences created a very dynamic, international business.

More and more businesses today recognize the value of positioning what they are doing to fill a needed economic gap or omission.

For example, a prominent auto muffler company, seeking to add secondary profit centers to its existing business, positioned its sales efforts among gas stations. It has currently signed up some 5000 gas stations as associates to whom it sells equipment to manufacture and sell mufflers.

Another company in the muffler field, Meineke Discount Mufflers, benefited from the term "discount" to provide it with the positioning that separated it from the established giants in the field.

WHALING SHIP CONCEPT

The old whaling ships often went out on sea voyages of 2 years or even longer before returning. As motivation, all members of the ship were given "a share of the catch" based on the official duties performed aboard the ship. Everyone, from the captain to able-bodied seamen, received shares.

The same principle can be applied in Branchising; for example, you can provide

a profit sharing plan to branch managers. Or you can establish a basic level of corporate earnings and, thereafter, grant "bonuses" based on earnings achieved beyond this figure. Each participant, from the manager to the clerks, receives varying shares.

This principle has been effectively applied in many areas, such as the fast-food field, the electronic parts industry, and other areas.

COMMISSION SALES AGENCY

The branch operator (Branchisee) provides, pursuant to this idea, a store and sales personnel. The Branchisor provides an exclusive territorial license to the Branchisee, as a sales agency of the company. The Branchisor also provides the floor inventory of the product to be displayed in the branch store. The Branchisee operates the store and takes orders which are submitted to and filled by the Branchisor. A commission check is forwarded by the Branchisor to the branch agency for all orders received. This "sales agency plan" comprises a low-cost distribution system with wide application.

While no charge is made for the sales agency license, as a practical matter, the agency must meet a certain sales quota or risk having its sales agency contract canceled. The Branchisor's normal profit on sales can be supplemented by training fees charged for indoctrinating the agency's personnel. The Branchisee covers the cost of store rental, personnel, and advertising. The primary cost to the Branchisor is the cost of the display inventory for the sales agency.

PROFIT SHARING PLAN

One approach to profit sharing is by stock ownership. Under this method the company's owners or stockholders divide the net profits equally among the common shares issued and outstanding. The result is known as "earnings per share" or "net profits per share." A portion of these earnings per share is distributed as dividends. In this way the owners or stockholders share in the profits of the corporation, according to their interest in the corporation.

This is basic profit sharing. However, the stockholders may desire to encourage the professional management of their corporation by permitting them to share in the profits without prior stock investment. One method for accomplishing this is to give these persons an option to purchase the shares of the company at a particular price, over a specified period of time. The price at which this stock is "optioned" is usually close to the market price of the shares at the time the option is granted. Hence, the option owner only benefits by an increase in the price of the shares resulting from increased earnings due to management's improved efficiency.

Start-up Plan Example

Basically, such profit sharing plans are bonus plans. The size of the bonus is related to the earnings produced by the manager of the particular unit.

As an example, a parent company has internally financed, created, and built one operating branch. As yet, no sales have been made. Here is the way the financing problem is approached:

The parent company retains 100 percent equity ownership of the branch unit.

The parent company reserves a 50 percent interest in future net profits for its own account.

A 20 percent interest in net profits is reserved for purchase by the unit's manager.

Six 5 percent interests in net profits are reserved for sale to other investors.

An upset price is established for the business in order to place a dollar price on the sale of the bonus interests. This may be arbitrarily arrived at by comparing the new unit with other similar units, or the company's capital investment may be added to estimated future annual profits to arrive at a value of individual bonus units.

After the first year of operation, the unit manager has the privilege of purchasing 5 percent interests in other properties, as such bonus interests become available. Should the operating manager be promoted to the position of district supervisor, he is then obligated to sell his 20 percent bonus interest, at the price he originally paid, to another working manager. He is then permitted to purchase 5 percent bonus interests in four other units, thereby reestablishing his 20 percent bonus interest in the company. These bonus interests would be calculated on net profits after taxes but before other charges, such as dividends. The parent company retains 100 percent equity interest in the property.

Profit Sharing Arrangement

In such a profit sharing arrangement, the sponsor tries to obtain long-term employees because this reduces training costs, increases efficiency, and enlarges the internal labor pool for potential senior management. Efficient long-term employees also tend to improve the quality and consistency of earnings.

The plan is based on the activation of a profit sharing arrangement plus the capital leverage of the managers' investment and the company's credit.

Through the operation of the Branchise plan, the parent company controls 50 percent of continuing profits with the balance of profits shared by a selected individual (having good management capability and receiving up to a 20 percent profit participation limit), absentee investors, insiders, and other network managers (5 percent interests). This plan is most suitable for those industries where it is difficult to obtain competent people because of the image of the business, high labor turnover, personnel problems, union problems, law suits, job boredom, and high capital investment requirements.

Under this arrangement, the manager just "manages" the unit but possesses more opportunity and freedom than were he just an employee. In addition, the usual franchise obligations are bypassed. The manager is freed from the responsibilities of ownership of plant, building, and equipment or the development of the business. The parent company handles all these functions.

High Net Profit Makes Plan Work

There is no equity or goodwill built up for the participant, as there is in the operation of a franchise. The combination of a low guaranteed salary and a high net profit makes the plan work. The manager gains more pride than were he solely an employee and, also, more security, depending upon the terms and conditions of termination and repurchase of his percentage interests. Therefore, he is apt to be more carefully selected, screened, and trained versus a "normal" employee. The manager's main interest is "What I can earn each month?" No equity that can be sold for a capital gain has been built up.

Should a manager desire to leave, or be "terminated," the parent company must return to the manager/investor his original investment, even with a bad unit.

This type of Branchising arrangement may not come under the franchising law, per se. In each state, the laws should be inspected, carefully, so that the securities laws are not violated.

The parent company often owns or has interest in supply firms, support operations, and centralized accounting systems (necessary to protect the company's 50 percent interest) and gets a management fee for supervision and purchasing services. The parent company has a written agreement with each unit to perform these services, for which it is reimbursed.

VARIATION OF A PROFIT SHARING ARRANGEMENT

Description of Plan

Young managers, in their mid-20s, are carefully interviewed several times (as dropout rate is high), and are trained and evaluated, frequently, over a 1.5- to 2-year period. Prior to becoming a manager, the candidate must invest $5000 to $7000 in his unit, for operating inventory.

Trainees are paid $140 to $180 a week, but for a manager the total income is all the money left over after paying store bills. Often there is a guaranteed income that covers him until he gets his operation running smoothly.

The parent company sells everything possible to the unit at a profit and has an assessment upon gross sales ranging between 5.6 to 12.7 percent. The manager can be promoted to higher-volume stores or new ones or to corporate staff.

Purpose of Plan

The company wants to maintain control, so franchising is not so appealing. Often this type of business does not have any unusual concept to distinguish it and does not have the usual potential of *high volume* and *high net profit* offered in the previously described arrangement. The money that can be made in this business lies basically in the *control of labor.* Therefore, the manager works many more hours, so the savings in labor is his. The average manager earns about $15,000 to $20,000. It is questionable whether a company store with a normal salaried manager would be a profitable entity.

As an incentive and to augment the sense of "participation" by the manager, a certain percentage of stock is set aside for option purposes. The number of people ready to take over managerships is a prime factor in getting the rate of expansion program.

INTERNATIONAL BRANCHISING: A MARKETING PLAN

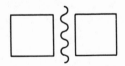

There is a huge, receptive international market for valid U.S. Branchises. The population of the eighteen "open" countries of Europe alone is now nearly double that of the United States, and their combined gross national product now exceeds $559 billion. A recent "business opportunities fair" attracted over 2000 prospective Branchisees, who were able to invest from $10,000 to $100,000. One investor group indicated the ability to raise $5 million to set up viable prototype operations.

A consistent inquiry voiced at the fair was "How can we get to know about the most feasible U.S. Branchises?" The following discussion summarizes the various Branchising methods used overseas and outlines one preferred method.

Many Branchisors have gone overseas this way:

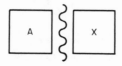

A represents the U.S. Branchisor. *X* represents the Branchisee that has been sold overseas, often for a substantial sum of "front money." This has not proved successful as a general rule because the overseas Branchisee was not truly a Branchisee. He was an "indigestible" entity who, in the long run, created problems and expense in excess of his investment, and then ended up by confiscating the entire program as his own. (We can name example after example.)

Others have gone abroad like this:

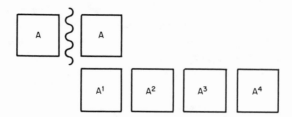

A is the U.S. Branchisor. The overseas *A* is the U.S. home office representative dispatched to the country to reside there and to establish a pilot operation. A^1, A^2, A^3, and A^4 represent his operational staff from the United States to implement the program. Such staffs can comprise as many as ten individuals.

The Problems with this Approach.   First, it becomes too costly (one fast-food operation spent nearly $250,000 on this format—yet failed). Second, it is generally commenced the wrong way. Usually it is copied directly from the prototype operation in the States. There has been no "reblending" to the attitudes and needs of the respective countries, which only native expertise can properly attain. Finally, a lack of knowledge of legalities, regulations, and restrictions in the various countries, e.g., zoning, licensing, construction sites, etc., can lead to legal difficulties.

Still other U.S. Branchisors have done it this way:
Again *A,* in this case, is the U.S. Branchisor. *X* is the master Branchisee who has been appointed overseas. *Y* and *Z* are regional Branchisees recruited by the master Branchisee.

46   BRANCHISING

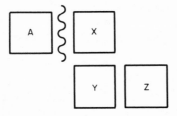

The Problem Here. The master Branchisee has never been properly indoctrinated. Nor does he have an adequate training and an operational organization to properly backup for the regional Branchisees. Hence, instead of a viable overseas Branchise program, the U.S. Branchisor has a number of component "particles," detached and insulated away.

The Preferred Way

1. The U.S. Branchisor appoints a resident director in each country.

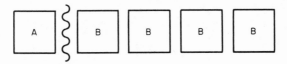

B represents the resident director. This director should be a well-financed, highly reputable executive with a proven background in government, marketing, and finance. He will have the following duties:

Help the U.S. Branchisor orient to each country.

Assist in needed program modifications including legalities.

Assist in readapting the U.S. Branchise "package," contractual agreements, and other needed projects.

Direct the search for and selection of suitable branch operators.

2. A master Branchisee in each country sets up his own prototype operation.

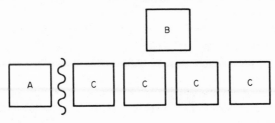

C is the master Branchisee appointed for your program in his particular country. He operates under the supervision of *B*, the resident director in his country. *C*, too, will be a well-financed executive and administrator of proven accomplishments. The appointment of such a Branchisee will have the following advantages:

The Branchisee will come to the states at his own expense for training from the Branchisor, thus equipping him to be the equivalent of a "sub-Branchisor" in his country.

He will establish a prototype operation in his country and—once this has been proven out—act to recruit regional Branchisees and thereafter train and maintain them (with the continuing consultation of the U.S. Branchisor).

He will own a big stake—a stake as big as the U.S. Branchisor himself—in the product or service being profitably sold in the foreign market.

He will have the capital, knowledge, and resources to develop a brand name orientation toward the American product or service in his market.

He will have a thorough knowledge of business methods in his market and the ability to adjust American procedures to fit the needs of a foreign market.

3. Each master Branchisee sets up all training and operations for expansion throughout his country.

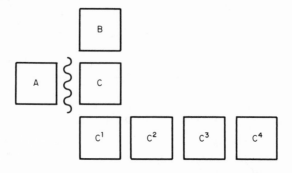

C^1, C^2, C^3, and C^4 represent the master Branchisee's training and operational staff. This becomes an in-depth organization that implements the needs of both the prototype operation and the subsequent Branchisees.

4. The master Branchisee then appoints and supervises all Branchisees in his country.

Here we have the ideal Branchising program for a foreign country. The overseas market director (*B*) and master Branchisee (*C*) not only have learned the techniques of the U.S. Branchisor but have adopted them for their own country. Thus once the training and operational staff is implemented, an endless series of profitable Branchisees follows (*D*'s).

48

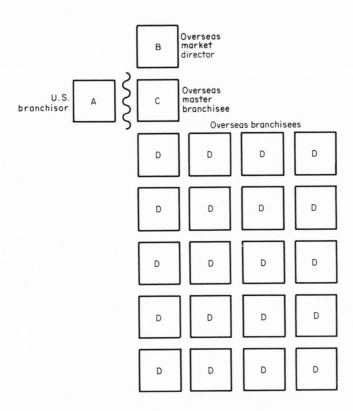

RECRUITMENT OF BOTH MASTER AND REGIONAL BRANCHISEES

One of the strengths of this program to U.S. Branchisors is the continuing Branchisee recruitment that can be generated—both master and regional. This is accomplished through the following:

1. A "business opportunities fair" approach, similar to one that attracted some 2000 investors in London

2. Access in each country to U.S. trade centers, cooperating by (a) extending the use of exhibit halls, (b) making business contacts, (c) extending the use of mailing lists, (d) publicity, and (e) special mailings

3. The cooperation in various countries of U.S. chambers of commerce, including access to their lists and person-to-person cooperation

4. Exposure through seminars before industrial organizations and other groups

5. Extensive publicity planned in the important Branchise and investment publications both in the United States and overseas (also in key metropolitan newspapers), conveying added invaluable exposure to prospective investors

Part
TWO

Structuring & Implementing the Branchise Program

Introduction

Part Two discusses how to structure and implement a Branchising program from its initial conceptual stages.

The "program-building" techniques contained herein are similar to the franchising concept—also a form of Branchising—both of which aim to provide effective procedures and tools to help their associates succeed.

PROGRAM-BUILDING STEPS

Generally speaking, structuring a Branchising program is done on a "block-on-block" basis, similar to constructing a high-rise building. Each block is interlinked with, and constitutes a foundation for, the next block.

These building blocks include:

1. **Feasibility assessment.** It's vital that you have checked out the feasibility of your product or service. (Pages 56–59 contain an eighteen-point, self-check feasibility criteria.)

2. **Preliminary research.** Take an objective across-the-street look at your business or program. Determine whether it has current applicability to new selected markets.

3. **Preparation of comprehensive blueprint.** This is the basic "plan" that details all program implementation procedures, provides step-by-step guidance, and prevents damaging omissions.

4. **Preparation of program "package."** This includes materials and services needed to recruit associates and to help them achieve success.

5. **Establishment of a prototype.** The prototype, in effect, is a pilot operation equated very closely with your planned branch units in both appearance and operational procedures. The objective of this prototype is to "prove out" the success of your operation, conforming to your expectations and representations.

6. **Program expansion.** Based on the success of the aforesaid prototypes, program expansion can now be undertaken. Initially, additional branch units are established in areas accessible to the parent; thereafter, expansion can be extended, ripplelike, to more and more areas.

TERMS USED IN PART TWO

For simplicity and quick absorbtion, the following terms are used in Part Two:

1. "Associate" is used to denote a Branchisee.
2. "Parent" is used to denote a Branchisor.

The Program

PROGRAM OBJECTIVES

To clearly plan any corporate undertaking, you must clearly define your goals or objectives and make provision for measuring the results obtained. Both initial and future objectives must be defined in order to permit reassessment and reevaluation as the program progresses. Flexibility must be built into the program in order to respond to change, additions, deletions, and modifications, which will improve the overall concept. At the same time, however, the long-range objective must be understood. The major objectives of a Branchise program can be divided into two phases.

The Successful Prototype

It is necessary to establish at least one successful prototype operation in accordance with the format which is presented here. The prototype will serve as:

1. A proving ground for the concepts, methods, and techniques established for the planned Branchising program
2. A secondary training center for the development of corporate administration and operational personnel
3. An additional pilot operation to provide the necessary income, expense, and profit documentation required for subsequent Branchise recruitment
4. An additional research and development center for the testing of all precepts, promotional programs, advertising programs, and similar programs

The Successful Expansion

When the prototype operations have achieved the desired level of success and the image and format are clearly established, the parent company is then in a position to proceed with subsequent objectives of the Branchise program:

1. To establish a nationwide network of Branchisees as quickly as practical, in accordance with the dictates of sound management practices

FOUR

2. To develop the executive staff and administrative procedures required for the efficient control and operation of the Branchised network

3. To create a modus operandi for Branchisee recruitment training, administration, and sales promotion—with reasonable assurance of achieving initial and long-range success for both the Branchisee and the parent company

4. To formulate the Branchise program to become self-sustaining within a minimum operational period

5. To increase net profits to the parent organization from both the sale of Branchises and the increased business produced by successfully operating Branchisees

6. To research other areas for additional sources of income; e.g., additional products and services may be offered to an established clientele by the Branchisees within their existing facilities and with a minimum of additional operating cost

While this proposal is designed as a practical, strategic plan for executing a profitable growth program, a degree of flexibility should always be maintained. Flexibility, in fact, is the key to meeting the unanticipated or special conditions that are bound to occur even in the most well-ordered approach. Therefore, while objectives and directions remain essentially unchanged, the tactics to meet them may have to be reconsidered from time to time. Methods must be subjected to continuous review, and the program, which leaves room for maneuvering, can be constantly modified.

EIGHTEEN-POINT FEASIBILITY CRITERIA

1. Is the success of your own organization a matter of record? Bear in mind that the Branchisee is buying your preproven success formula, plus your ability and commitment to extend this record to a new market area through the Branchisee.

2. Does your company have a record of financial stability? Sound financial status is also necessary to attract and support qualified Branchisees. It is important to remember that to the Branchisee your company assumes a "parental" role. The Branchisee desires to be reassured that your company is an enduring factor in the industry and will not fail because of undercapitalization.

3. Is your company in a secure position in its industry? Do you have a reasonable share of the available market? Do you believe that this market share can be increased?

4. Your products or services should be analyzed objectively. Does your product or service have enduring customer appeal? Does an element of distinctiveness exist? This does not mean, necessarily, a completely different type of product or service than is available in the present market. Such distinctiveness can also lie in packing, merchandising, servicing, or in structural format. However, it should give to the consumer something different that is not available from competitive products or services.

5. A product or service "repeat" factor is highly desirable. Recall the "oil for the lamps of China" theory; whereunder, the lamps are distributed free in order to

generate the repeat oil business. Or the "razor–razor blade" concept. Such repeat patronage elements in a product or service tend to create an "annunity" type of business, as compared to the single-sale concept.

6. Does your product or service enjoy an inherently good profit margin? Can the business support a reasonable standard of living? The quality of Branchisees attracted to your program can vary in direct proportion to the believability and size of the profit potential.

7. Your business may seem simple to you; after all, you probably created it, or, at the least, you have probably operated for many years in your field. So it may come as a surprise to have to ask yourself: Is the product or service "trainable"? Can a Branchisee having little or no experience in your field operate successfully? Can you possibly teach him to do so? Interestingly, it has been found that those experienced in nonrelated fields normally absorb training more easily and perform better than the trainee who has had experience in your particular industry.

8. Can your product or service be projected into a national market? Or has it only regional acceptance? If it can operate in a national market, do you have sufficient supply sources so that you can service Branchisees, efficiently and economically, in any part of the country?

9. Is an installation requirement linked to the sale of your product? If so, can such installation be "farmed out" to local tradespeople or technicians? Can the installation be accomplished at a reasonable, predetermined price?

10. Are freight costs an important element in the sale of your product? Must you ship heavy or bulky products? Will excessive freight charges reduce profits? Will regional warehousing, with minimum full-carload area shipments required, solve the problem?

11. Do you have sufficient capacity of unused production to meet a sharp increase in sales? You can be "killed," literally, by an unforeseen success. As a classic example of this, there was a franchisor operating in the infrared-heating field. All went even better than expected: The first franchisee group produced $1 million in sales, in short order. The franchisor was not able to handle this volume, was unable to subcontract, and the expected acquisition of a larger factory, with which to increase production, failed to materialize. The result was "failure due to success."

12. What is the depth of your personnel? Do you have sufficient personnel with the ability to administer a Branchise program? Or is your present staff busy handling the normal workload of your business? If the latter is the case, you must expand your staff to meet new program requirements. At a minimum you will require a Branchise director, and as your Branchisee acquisition rate grows, you must be ready to add personnel in the areas of administration, field contact, and operations control.

13. Is there a viable financing plan? In most franchised operations, financing generally depends upon these factors (which also pertain to Branchising): (1) land, (2) structure, (3) equipment, (4) inventory, and (5) modernization.

Such financing, ordinarily, is accomplished through any, or combination, of the following:

a. *Franchisor.* He will finance the structure, lease, or inventory.

b. *Lessor.* In many instances, the lessor will subordinate his land and/or build to suit. Builders and contractors will also build to suit, based on a prescribed percentage or rental yield.

c. *Local banks.* They may know the franchisee and the business potential of a neighborhood franchise.

d. *Governmental lending sources.* Organizations such as SBA, FHA, and HUD can grant loans. Their loans have been minimal, recently, but may become available more easily, in the future.

e. *Franchise lease insurance.* The franchisee lease is guaranteed for its entire term, thereby relieving the franchisor from a substantial contingent liability. This type of lease insurance is available through a number of SBA-associated firms.

f. *Private investment sources.* These sources include SBICs, insurance companies, private investors, and private syndicates. Syndicate investors are frequently comprised of professional groups, such as physicians, dentists, and accountants, who are receptive to absentee ownership and possibly certain tax advantages. The latter method has been used with motels, nursing homes, and other large investment franchises.

g. *Minority group financing.* This is geared to help minorities, i.e., the MESBIC program, which involves private investors operating under special governmental dispensation.

14. What is the growth position of your industry? What percentage of your market has been saturated? Is your industry's annual compounded growth rate progressively higher, or is your industry mature and showing signs of decline? Naturally, an industry with a minimum of postmarket exploitation and an excellent expansion potential is more desirable for a franchise program.

15. Can you maintain your competitive position? You may be strong in your regional market, but can you be equally strong in another market area which may already be dominated by a national operator? Can you compete there? How will you go about it?

16. Are your profit projections realistic? What is your present share of the market? Do you have sufficient capital and managerial competence to expand your share of the market at the same profit margins you have engaged in the past, or will you have to price cut to enter the new market? Are your growth rates sound? Has your present operation demonstrated that your growth projections are within the realm of possible achievement?

17. Most importantly, what is your reputation with the consumer? It is this consumer acceptance which places a market value on your trademark. Do you have above-average consumer acceptance in your present operating area, as evidenced by a minimum of product returns and progressively higher annual sales totals?

18. Lastly, are you philosophically ready to become a Branchisor? Are you ready to give up some business independence for the good of your branch network? What is your objective in entering Branchising? Is it short range or long range? Normally, a Branchisor should not expect profits from the initial branch fee. These funds should merely reimburse the Branchisor for expenses incurred for materials and services given to the Branchisee. The larger profits are longer term in nature and derive from the multiplicity of successful Branchisees, developed by the parent organization. On the other hand, the fee for the initial Branchise program should be sufficient so that the Branchisor can meet his obligations to the branch network with ease.

If you can answer most of the foregoing questions positively, the next step is to consider exactly what constitutes the "building blocks" of a good Branchise program.

Figure 4-1 is an example of a PERT, or critical path chart, depicting the step-by-step procedures for implementing a Branchising program from the initial stages.

PROGRAM BLUEPRINT

The program blueprint for Branchising is a comprehensive "preplan" that evaluates and projects all elements of the envisaged program including:

1. Selected program format
2. Type of Branchisee sought (qualifications, detailed criteria)
3. The program "package" (what it should include from the standpoint of structure, materials, services, etc.)
4. Arithmetical projections

The projections are an estimate of what it costs to implement the program and how these costs are reimbursed. Such reimbursements come from the initial Branchise fee and ongoing, residual income. Ongoing, residual income refers to continuing services. The Branchise fee refers to initial costs incurred in the establishment of a Branchising unit: recruitment costs (advertising, sales, etc.), package costs (literature and materials that are supplied), training expenses, administrative costs, grand-opening program, and other expenses.

The blueprint also assesses and defines:

1. Estimated numbers of associates to be recruited over a period of 5 years, pertinent expenses and income, and resultant "bottom line" net profit
2. Area allotment
3. Advertising and promotions
4. Training procedures

A Branchise blueprint should detail every facet and procedure of the total program, in depth. The following pages contain a table of contents of a typical program. Its thoroughness of preplanning is reflected.

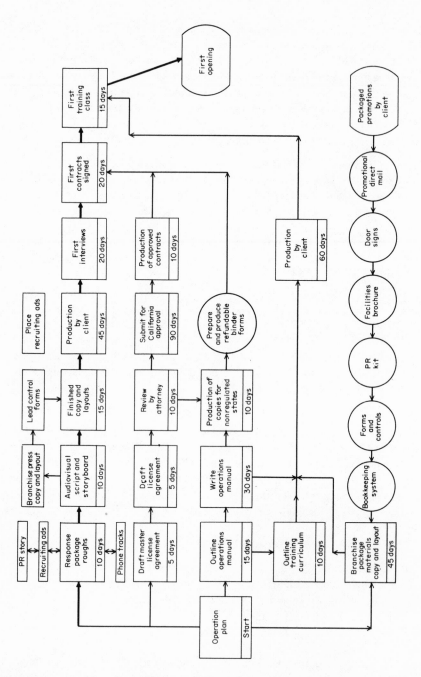

Figure 4-1 Example of a PERT, or critical path, chart depicting the step-by-step procedures for implementing a Branchising program from its initial stages.

BRANCHISING

A Sample Branchise Blueprint

Contents*

PREMISES

General information

Population required to support a hamburger drive-in

Individual location determination

Location forms—general information

Real estate preliminary survey

Building analysis form

Location point evaluation form

Site certification form

Survey outline form

Location approving and securing form

Utility gas form

Utility water form

Utility electric form

Utility service form

General completion check form

Site analysis form

Construction check sheet form

Basic site requirements explained

Methods of acquiring hamburger drive-in locations

---

*Note logical progression and detail. The following sample was designed for the organization of a hamburger drive-in system.

LEGAL REQUIREMENTS

Legal documents, general information
Transactions requiring legal documents
Preliminary branchise agreement
Preliminary branchise escrow agreement
Preliminary agreement of location
Preliminary agreement of location escrow agreement
Preliminary agreement for territorial license
Preliminary agreement of license escrow agreement
Branchise agreement
Territorial license agreement
Ground lease
Ground sublease
Improved lease for building leasebacks
Improved sublease
Thirty legal documents for fast-food drive-in transactions
Legal documents for closing a sale

BUILDING AND CONSTRUCTION

Building, general information
Plot plan and layout data
Parking plan and layout data
Construction methods of a hamburger turnkey project
Ninety blueprints of structure
Building specifications—50 pages, plus

EQUIPMENT

Equipment, general information
Itemized lists of hamburger drive-in equipment
List of griddle manufacturers
List of fryer manufacturers
List of shake machine manufacturers
List of soft drink dispenser manufacturers
List of ice machine manufacturers
List of cooler manufacturers
List of freezer manufacturers
List of coffee maker manufacturers
Complete set of blueprints for special stainless steel equipment
Itemized list of custom-fabricated, stainless steel, hamburger equipment packages
Wholesale price lists of hamburger equipment packages
Griddle, specifications and prices
Fryer, specifications and prices
Shake machines, specifications and prices
Freeze shake machine, specifications and prices
Soft drink dispensers, specifications and prices
Ice machine, specifications and prices
Walk-in cooler, specifications and prices
Coffee maker, specifications and prices
Potato peeler, specifications and prices
Cash register, specifications and prices
Shake, holding cabinet, specifications and prices
Metal master sink, specifications and prices
Lists of alternative equipment, other manufacturers' specifications and prices
Equipment layout plans and utilities connections

Master list of all equipment, specifications, prices, wholesale and retail

Itemized list of small equipment "package"

General equipment data

SIGNS

Signs, general information
Description and application of signs
Blueprint of signs

List of sign manufacturers including addresses
Interior menu signs
Sign prices, wholesale and retail

OPERATIONS

Operations Manual

Sections

1. Hamburger drive-in food service
   Preopening:
   a. Installation of equipment
   b. Duties of owner and manager
   c. Equipment
   d. Additional construction projects
   e. Additional equipment and supplies
   f. Food production
   g. Preparation of food products
2. Opening the store
3. Manager
4. Opening procedures
5. Closing procedures
6. One week before opening
7. Four days before opening
8. Additional food items
9. Operating procedure
10. Cleaning procedure
11. Ordering procedure
12. Ordering paper supplies
13. Inventory control
14. Damaged merchandise
15. Advertising
16. Safety procedure
17. Cleaning and maintenance schedule
18. Uniforms
19. Pilferage
20. Spoilage and waste
21. Profits
22. Sixteen operating forms, e.g., daily, weekly, monthly
23. Food and paper cost analysis (e.g., patty papers 0.0008)
24. Initial miscellaneous articles and supplies
25. Food supplies list
26. Paper supplies list
27. Miscellaneous supplies list
28. Office supplies list
29. Cleaning supplies list
30. List of all supply costs

ADVERTISING AND PROMOTION PROGRAM

Advertising, general information
Advertising mats
Advertising manual
Grand-opening program

Public relations in the trading area
"Tie-ins" with local industry
Obtaining local publicity
Continuing promotions

BOOKKEEPING, FINANCE, CORPORATE ORGANIZATION

Bookkeeping, general information
Bookkeeping for a hamburger drive-in
operation
Bookkeeping, manual and forms
Financing, general information
Financing, signs-all methods
Financing the Branchisee
Financing the equipment, all methods
Financing the building
Financing methods used for hamburger

drive-ins
Corporate organization of a hamburger
drive-in
Corporate organization for financing a
branch
Corporate organization for a hamburger
drive-in leasing and development op-
eration
Corporate organization for a territorial
Branchise company

GENERAL INFORMATION

Costs, general information (wholesale
and retail):
   equipment costs
   sign costs
   supplies costs
   initial costs
Projected profits analysis
Actual profits analysis
Literature of competing hamburger
chains
Image, decor, and theme

Name, colors, and atmosphere
The market, customers, population and
types
Money- and labor-saving methods and
devices
Methods and procedures of territorial
Branchising, selling, and licensing
Sales brochure
History and development of the ham-
burger drive-in
List of hamburger drive-in operations

TABLE OF ORGANIZATION

A successful Branchising program must have an adequate "table of organization." This "table" refers to the structuring of corporate personnel—on both executive and subordinate levels—to effectively fulfill the commitments of this type of program.

Such a table of organization is elastic, and *stretches* to conform to the recruitment pace and other needs.

The following pages contain examples of tables of organization for a hypothetical Branchising program. Initially, one person is designated the "branch director." He constitutes the liaison with the branch operators and the parent company executives. His functions include:

1. Consultation relative to preparation of the program "package"
2. Accumulation of necessary data and material needed to expedite the program
3. Consultation relative to operator recruitment procedures
4. Responsibility for ordering and scheduling the necessary operator equipment included within the branch package
5. Supervision of training school
6. Supervision of operator field support
7. Acting as a communication center for both the branch recruitment salespeople and prospective branch operators, while representing the home office

As the program progresses, new people and offices are added to keep pace with operator recruitment. These include additional field people and administrative assistants, as shown in Figure 4-2.

ORGANIZATION PLANNING AND STRUCTURING

Manpower Scheduling

The table of organization (Figure 4-2) projects the optimum organization structure as recommended during the first 2 years. The prospective input of manpower into this organization on a scheduled quarterly basis is shown in Figures 4-3 and 4-4.

Phase I. At the time that the entire Branchise package is completed, the manpower should be implemented as scheduled in Figure 4-3. The Branchising director must be appointed within the first month of operations in order to direct activities at the outset. The Branchising director will thereupon hire a secretary. Meanwhile, recruiting ads will have been placed in the appropriate media to attract potential Branchisees.

The parent organization will be operational but without any more manpower input until the third quarter. Projected operator sales indicate that five branches should be sold by the close of the third quarter. At this point it is determined that a training

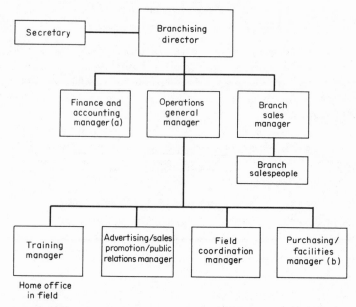

Figure 4-2 Table of organization. *Note:* The finance and accounting manager *(a)* is responsible for financial planning and controls, accounting (home office), and reports (financial and statistical). The purchasing/facilities manager *(b)* oversees equipment and purchasing supplies, site location, plant layout, and grand opening.

manager's services would be required. An additional three branch sales are projected within the fourth quarter.

During the fourth quarter, it is expected that the volume of activity will increase substantially in the financial aspects of the business. Therefore, the manager of finance and accounting is phased into the operation in the fourth quarter of the first year.

As the workload reaches a point when the present management cannot handle the volume, responsibilities must be subdivided and additional positions created and filled. What we have done, within Figures 4-2 to 4-4, is design an optimum organization and fill each position as the need develops.

Phase II. Figure 4-4 indicates phase II of manpower scheduling which takes place during the second year of operation of the Branching program.

In the first quarter of the second year, an additional four branch sales are projected, the total projection being twelve branches in various stages of operation. After a branch becomes operational, the need for its quick and total exposure to the potential marketplace is important. Much of this is accomplished through advertising, sales promotions, and public relations. It becomes necessary to hire the manager of advertising, sales promotion, and public relations to assume these responsibilities during the second quarter of the second year.

In the second year's first quarter, the manager of purchasing and branch facilities is needed. His function is to provide the following types of services:

Grand opening—planning and scheduling

Equipment purchasing and leasing

Printing of stationery, forms, cards, etc.

Coordination of reports, statistical data, earnings, etc.

Interpretation of reports to operators and the manager of field activities

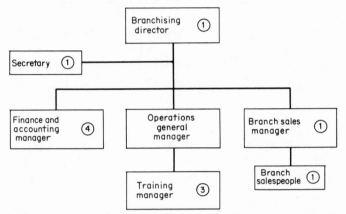

Figure 4-3 Manpower scheduling chart—phase I, year I. Circled numbers refer to the quarter in which the position is filled.

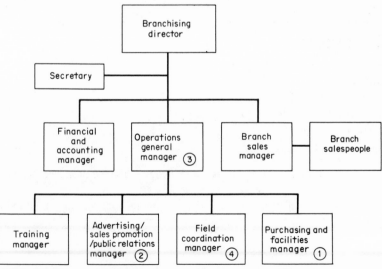

Figure 4-4 Manpower scheduling chart—phase II, year II. Circled numbers refer to the quarter in which the position is filled.

The manager of field activities coordination is hired in the fourth quarter of the second year. His responsibility is completely involved with how effectively the owner/managers are operating. It is his function to work with any implementation of new programs as they are developed by the manager of advertising, sales promotion, and public relations, as well as new concepts developed by the management for an operator's use and/or expansion. He must be aware of what each operator is doing and assist him in becoming more efficient and productive. He assists in the initial field training of each new owner/manager and the "grand-opening" phase of the new branch.

In the third quarter, the Table of Organization is completed by the hiring of the general manager of operations. The general manager of operations is primarily concerned with that phase of the business which starts after a new branch is acquired. He provides the operator with orientation, training, grand-opening technique, servicing, and scheduled field visits. It is the general manager of operation's responsibility to be aware of the internal and external factors which affect the growth potential of the branch manager organization.

The general manager of operations should assume his duties as soon as possible. He should be totally involved in the formative phases of the branch program in order to be more completely aware of the needs and directions of both the parent company and the operator.

At the stage when the branch director appoints the general manager of operations, there is a projected total of twenty branches that have been sold and become operational. Thus, the director of Branchising may need a "buffer" of management personnel to handle the day-to-day operators' organization, and he should become more deeply involved in the following plans and decisions:

Profit and loss of the organization

Reasons for profit and/or loss

The need for additional capital

Rate of expansion

New programs to increase branch sales

New businesses

Investment of income

This schedule of manpower needs is directly related to the projected branch sales within the first 2 years of operations.

Table 4-1 is a projected wage schedule for the personnel who will fill the manpower schedule.

TABLE 4-1 A Projected Wage Scale for Manpower Scheduling on a Quarterly Basis

	Recommended starting salaries*	
First year quarters	Annual	Quarterly
1. Director of Branchising	$20,000	$5,000
2. Secretary	10,000	2,500
3. Training manager	16,000	4,000
4. Manager of finance and accounting	18,000	4,500
Second year quarters		
1. Manager of advertising, sales promotion, and public relations	16,000	4,000
2. Manager of purchasing and Branchisee facilities	15,000	3,750
3. General manager of operations	18,000	4,500
4. Manager of field activities coordination	16,500	4,125

*These recommended wages vary relative to location, program status, company status, etc.

ORGANIZATIONAL JOB DESCRIPTIONS

Positions of Responsibility

The organization as shown in Figure 4-2 is further clarified by a description of the job content of each managerial position. These descriptions will hereafter be referred to as "positions of responsibility." Within each position of responsibility, you will note the following divisions:

Job title (position)

Reporting level

Common responsibilities

Administrative and managerial duties

Common Responsibilities *should represent all employees, be it operator or managerial*

Since the "common responsibilities" are the same for every manager, they are listed before the actual positions of responsibility.

1. Participate in the development of policies of the company, and interpret such policies throughout the organization and to all operators.

2. Develop objectives, policies, and procedures for the organization subject to the approval of his superior.

3. Interpret and administer programs and procedures for the organization in accordance with approved policies.

5. Develop expense budget objectives for the operation of the organization; require performance within budget.

5. Develop a suitable successor, and be responsible for the training of managerial replacements at all levels of the organization.

6. Constantly evaluate the organizational plan, corporate objectives, manpower planning, management appraisal, and budget controls as they relate to performance and goal achievement within the scope of company policies.

7. Perform special assignments for superiors, and function on "special committees" in accordance with the organization's need of his talents.

Model Positions of Responsibility

Here are two examples of positions of responsibility, describing the president's and the general manager of operation's functions.

PRESIDENT

Reporting level:

Common responsibilities: As indicated on pages 69–70.

Administrative and managerial duties:

He is responsible for:

- The overall branch operation of both company-owned stores and future branch stores in accordance with their needs to function effectively, efficiently, and profitably
- Providing the branch operator with the grand-opening program and assuring its implementation
- Marketing, advertising, sales promotion, marketing research, public relations, and similar programs in the development and operation of the branch business
- Being the principal spokesperson for the parent company and helping to promote and advance the most favorable public image possible
- Developing meaningful and sound relationships with members of the financial community, local and regional
- Developing additional sources for company and branch financing and exploring the means of increasing the availability of these financial sources for the operator
- New business development, as well as new market development, in the sale of the company's products throughout company-owned stores, branch stores, and other distribution channels
- The finance department, internal accounting, payroll, auditing of franchisee accounts, budget control, forms control, and cost reduction programs

GENERAL MANAGER OF OPERATIONS

Reporting level: Reports to president

Common responsibilities: As indicated on pages 69–70.

Administrative and managerial duties:

He is responsible for:

- Coordinating all the activities within the operator's organization
- Final approval of site location with the advice of the manager of field operations
- Layout planning
- Purchasing and installing furniture, fixtures, and equipment
- Providing all the materials, assistance, and direction necessary to assure that an operation becomes profitable, efficient, and effective
- Training and working closely with the training manager to accomplish the following:

  Recruiting qualified personnel to staff the restaurant

  Training the employees to handle efficiently the restaurant operations

  Reviewing operations training material and making recommendations for changes and improvements, stressing efficiency

  Assisting the training manager in establishing training procedures for the operators when new products, methods, or promotional programs are developed
- Frequent contact in person, by phone, or mail with each branch manager in order to have a constant knowledge of the operational problems within the total organization
- The preparation of the monthly operations reports on each operator for the president
- Directing a research and development program to seek out improved methods of providing services to the operators and their clients
- Developing techniques for the efficient handling and control of inventory
- Being a member of the committee organized to evaluate branch manager performance
- Reporting the status of each branch manager's operations
- Being able to work with his subordinate managers to solve all problems of communications, administration, promotion, and supply before they reach a crises stage

Positions of Responsibility in General

Although the preceding two positions of responsibility were given in great detail, you may prefer a more casual method. Here is a general approach for describing two positions of responsibility:

Training Manager

The "training manager" is responsible for the administration and effective application of the entire branch-training program. This includes supervision of the home office training schools as well as the training and supervision of the operations manager and/or the field supervisors. The training manager is required to establish standard field-training procedures and be responsible for seeing that these procedures are properly transmitted to the managers.

He makes periodic visits to the operators in conjunction with regional meetings in order to meet the operators in their designated areas. During these meetings he ascertains the effectiveness of the training program and obtains all the information necessary to institute needed improvements and modifications. He promptly notifies the branch director of any inefficiencies in the training program.

The training manager is also responsible for the development of the indoctrination techniques of the operators in any new programs which emanate from the research and development section of the corporate organization.

Manager of Advertising, Sales Promotion, and Public Relations

The "manager of advertising, sales promotion, and public relations" reports directly to the general manager of operations and is charged with responsibility for the maintenance of all established sales promotion and advertising schedules. The latter includes the development of annual national-advertising campaigns and promotions in cooperation with the operators in the various regions. He also assists and gives direction to the operators in all areas of advertising, sales promotion, and public relations in their local territories. He administers all of the special sales promotion plans.

Prior to general dissemination to the branch network, it is essential that all techniques are tried and proven at the home office.

Accurate and complete records must be maintained to assist in the analysis and improvement of all advertising and promotion.

Clerical Descriptions

Another category is simply called a "clerical description" because it applies to those positions which do not have managerial and administrative responsibilities, and thus, no common responsibilities. These positions simply indicate the duties assigned to these jobs. The secretarial position falls into this category.

Branch Secretary

The "branch secretary's" primary responsibilities include responding to all operator inquiries and transmitting the prospects' material to the branch salespeople. He also maintains the Branchising prospect's files and the recruiting and advertising analysis forms. Methods and procedures, including the controls necessary for maintaining complete, up-to-date records, should be established for the branch secretary. In addition, the branch secretary will perform all duties as secretary and assistant to the branch director.

Utilization of Job Descriptions

The job descriptions have many uses to management executives:

1. The description is to be used by the hiring organization to assist them in locating the type of individual it requires to perform the functions for which he will be hired. If additional specifications are needed, the job description ("position of responsibility") will provide management with its basic needs to expand upon these specifications to ensure proper screening. (Employment agencies specializing in executive personnel can perform this function very efficiently for home office management.)

2. A copy of the "position of responsibility" should be given to the person who is hired or promoted to a new position. This will provide him with the necessary knowledge needed to perform his job.

3. The job description can be used as a basic tool to appraise subsequent job performance of the employee.

4. Job performance appraisals can be used to control promotions and salary increases—they become the tools of management which determine personnel effectiveness.

ADVISORY COMMITTEE

The establishment of an "advisory committee" by the parent company can result in many benefits, including the added "documentation" based on the number of influential, prestigious persons acting as advisors to the branch program. The advisory committee also contributes varying expert points of view relative to new developments, current problems, operator communications, and similar subjects.

Members of this committee should be "individuals of influence and prestige" in the fields of banking (e.g., a bank president), education (e.g., a college professor), commerce (e.g., president or executive officer of a well-known business), and so on.

Individuals of this caliber are often responsive to membership on such a committee. It's flattering; it gives valuable exposure to new fields on a consultant level; and they look forward to being part of the "team" and participating with other individuals of influence.

In most instances, too, they will participate for minimal compensation. For example, an "honorarium" of $50 was paid for each meeting by one company that projected six meetings a year.

WHAT A BRANCHISE "PACKAGE" COMPRISES

A Branchise "package" comprises all the things which a parent company promises or gives to a Branchisee in return for the initial money paid. It consists of the kinds of "tools" needed (1) to make the Branchisee successful and (2) to recruit Branchisees.

Tools Needed to Make the Branchisee Successful

Operations Manual. This constitutes the program's "Bible," which is easily accessible for continual reference. It sets forth every detail of the operation and the recommended sales procedures. It recapitulates the instruction given to the Branchisee during schooling. The operations manual is also made part of the contract with the Branchisee, defining and controlling the manner in which the business must be operated and setting forth the Branchisee's commitments to the parent company and the parent company's commitments to the Branchisee.

Sales Presentation Book. This is an important tool, which may also be audio-visual, that illustrates and describes the benefits of the parent's services. It is used by the Branchisee in contacting prospective customers.

Advertising and Promotions. This varies, of course, depending on the nature of the products or services. However, it should include:

A grand-opening campaign

Direct mail (to be sent to prospective customers in an area)

"Newspaper advertising mats" (recommended ads for placement in local newspapers)

A publicity and public relations campaign (publicity write-ups for placement in local newspapers)

"Leave-behind" brochures (describing products or services)

Sales Manuals. These convey recommended selling techniques.

Simplified Bookkeeping System. Such a system enables the Branchisee to keep proper records. It also enables the parent company to have accessible records pertinent to royalties due.

Tools Needed to Recruit Branchisees

Recruitment Presentation Book. This dramatizes and documents the benefits of the program to prospective Branchisees.

Recruitment Brochure. A descriptive booklet, relative to the program, is sent generally in response to inquiries from prospective Branchisees.

Branchise Agreement. This should be prepared as compactly as possible and reflect all current legalities. It should also be oriented toward "affirmatives," the things that the parent company will do for the Branchisee, but should not overemphasize the things that the Branchisee cannot do.

Recruitment Control and Flow Forms. These forms provide a record of prospect leads that you receive and from what source. Also, they provide a record of when prospects were contacted and the results of these contacts.

Table of Organization. This is vital. You must have the personnel available to properly support the program at each stage. At the outset a branch director is necessary; he is, in effect, the program implementor. As Branchisees are recruited, other personnel should be phased in—both operational and administrative—to handle the needs.

BASIC EXPENSES OF A BRANCHISE PROGRAM

The next question may be "What does it cost to establish a Branchise program?" There are three basic types of expenses: (1) initial capital outlay, (2) recurring expenses, and (3) reserve capital.

The initial capital outlay is necessary to structure the program effectively. The recurring expenses are your day-to-day costs. Reserve capital is required to meet most regulations today. It also proves your financial solidity and proves the availability of adequate funds to fulfill your commitments to the branch managers.

The proper Branchise program—properly equipped and implemented—can help achieve outstanding marketing results and very substantial earnings. However, it is a definite requirement that the program should be established on a sound foundation with enough capital, effective sales tools, and administrative ability.

Financing

Most beginning branch operators need additional capital. Generally, the money they've accumulated to enter their own business is somewhat short of actual needs. Money is needed for:

Branchise fees

Property construction or improvements

Grand-opening program

Advertising and promotion

At least 6 months of working capital will be required prior to the attainment of the break-even point.

Established branch operators, too, often need additional financing. For example, money is needed for desired business expansion (added personnel, property improvements, or acquiring a second territory). It is also needed for increased advertising and promotional activity, seasonal financing, and inventory expansion.

The question paramount in their minds is "Where can I obtain this needed capital —on reasonable terms?"

Today, money is extremely "tight." Sources which were formerly responsive to loan requests have now, literally, "dried up." Hence the branch operator has less likelihood of obtaining favorable loans than in the past.

Your main loan source is generally the one most accessible to you: your nearby bank or savings and loan association. Being local, they are acquainted with you and your business and are familiar with your character, integrity, and stability. The guide they use for granting a loan is symbolized by "3 C's": character, capital, and capacity to pay.

BANK LOANS

Most banks, under normal circumstances, will make a reasonable loan to you. A bank loan is most advantageous because the interest rate is generally lowest.

You may obtain various types of loans from your local bank, as follows: (1) short-term loans (payable in about 90 days) or (2) long-term loans (extending for as long as 10 years).

"Popular" types of bank loans are listed below.

FIVE

Straight Commercial Loans. Based on your financial statement, they are usually from 30 to 60 days and are generally used for seasonal financing or inventory expansion.

Installment Loans. These are usually long-term loans, repayable on a monthly basis. They can be "tailored" to business needs, for example, heavier repayments during peak months and smaller repayments during off-season periods.

Term Loans. Such loans have maturities of 1 to 10 years and may either be secured or unsecured. Loan repayments may be made on almost any agreed-upon basis: monthly, quarterly, semiannually, or annually. Early repayments are often relatively small, and the loan ends with a large final payment. Although many term loans are secured with collateral, the lender requires ordinarily that current assets exceed current liabilities by at least a 2-1 ratio.

Bills or Notes Receivable. Promissory notes are often given for the purchase of goods. These notes are called "bills receivable" or "notes receivable." Usually, these can be discounted—that is, purchased by the bank. The seller's account is credited with the amount of the note less the discount to due date. The bank will collect from the note makers when it's due.

Warehouse Receipt Loans. Under this form of financing, goods are stored in a warehouse, and the warehouse receipt is given to the bank as security for a loan to pay the supplier. As fast as the borrower is able to sell his merchandise, he buys back portions of the warehoused inventory.

Equipment Loans. Loans are made to finance the purchase of machinery or equipment. The lender usually retains title until the installment payments have been completed.

Collateral Loans. These are based on such collateral as chattel mortgages on personal property, real estate mortgages, life insurance (up to cash surrender value of the policy), or stocks and bonds.

ALTERNATIVE LOANS

If your banker says "no," then contact your local Small Business Administration Office (SBA). They are organized to expedite loans (that are justifiable) for small businesses. They ask, as the first step, that the loan request originate with your local bank. If the bank refuses your loan request, the SBA will undertake, in many instances, to "share" your loan with the local bank and assume responsibility for 50 percent or more. The majority of banks (even those refusing your initial loan request) will usually cooperate with SBA-sponsored loans.

Another good loan source is the *Small Business Investment Company* (SBIC). SBIC uses partly private and partly federal money to provide capital for small businesses by means of loans, direct stock purchases, or debenture bonds convertible into stock.

This gives you a loan procurement opportunity formerly available only to larger companies. Approximately 480 SBICs are now in operation. Their financing costs are generally higher than banks but often lower than outside "private" sources. To obtain the names and addresses of SBICs in your area, write to:

Small Business Administration   National Association of SBICs
Investment Division   or   537 Washington Building
Washington, D.C. 20025   Washington, D.C. 20005

Here are some other avenues open to you for obtaining loans:

Private Capital. Insert an ad in your local newspaper under "Capital Wanted." Through this medium you may attract private investors who regularly consult this column for investment opportunities.

Factors. In each community there are factoring firms which make loans to all types of businesses. Their loan standards are lower than banks; hence they are more inclined to grant your loan (even though you may have been refused by banks or governmental sources). Factors are recommended only as a "last resort" since their interest rates are often onerous.

Veterans Administration Loans. If you are a veteran (either of World War II or the Korean war), you may be eligible to obtain a loan via your local Veterans Administration Office. Write to them to obtain their detailed pamphlet on the types of loans offered and their controlling regulations.

Insurance Companies. Many insurance companies maintain loan departments as an important adjunct to their business. Their rates (although generally higher than banks) are usually lower than that of factors and other loan sources.

Commercial Investment Companies. There are many investment companies, privately constituted, which grant loans. You will find them listed in your local telephone directories *(Yellow Pages)*. Their rates are generally on a par with the rates of factoring organizations.

Leasing Firms. "Leasing" has become more and more prominent in recent years. Almost any type of product or equipment can be leased now. Leases may be used to finance many aspects of your business, e.g., furniture, fixtures, machinery, or equipment. Such leases give you a period of 3 to 5 years to pay back (via small monthly payments). Another use is to finance your customers (particularly if your product cost is comparatively high). You (as the seller) are immediately paid the full amount due. The customer pays the leasing company monthly over a period of years.

Branchise "Package" Financing. Often, your Branchise package includes products and equipment which are "Branchiseable" (usually to the extent of 60 percent of the wholesale cost).

Floor Plan Financing. These are usually short-term loans applicable to merchandise in your store (on the floor), for example, boats, autos, appliances, and similar items.

ESOT AND ESOP FINANCING PLAN

Something new has developed in finance: the ESOP and the ESOT. These are methods of increasing working capital by using internal sources which, heretofore, have not been available and of having the possibility of recapturing past tax payments.

An ESOP is an "employee stock ownership plan." It allows employees to purchase previously issued stock retained live in the treasury or to purchase newly issued shares.

An ESOT is an "employee stock ownership trust." Such trusts are the depository for employer contributions, investments, accumulations, accruals, and income under the "plan." The trustee holds these assets and invests them according to the instructions of an investment committee.

To organize an ESOP, the company creates an ESOT. This trust then borrows funds from a bank and uses these loan proceeds to purchase a block of company stock.

The bank makes the loan to the trust because the loan is guaranteed by the company. In addition, the company agrees to pay the trust annual contributions of sufficient magnitude to repay the loan's principal and interest over the loan's life.

As the bank loan is repaid by the trust, the trusteed shares are allocated to employees in proportion to their payments, but these shares continue to be held by the trust. Only when a worker retires or leaves the company is it possible for him to obtain physical possession of the stock certificates. At that time, should no market exist for the company's shares, they will be purchased by the company or the trust.

The operating effect of the plan is as follows:

1. Employer contributions to the ESOP are tax deductible. In effect, the company has sold a block of its stock without paying any underwriting commissions. Also, the company pays a business loan and takes a tax deduction as to both principal and interest.
2. It obtains new financing which is repaid in pretax dollars.
3. It can obtain a refund of taxes paid in prior, profitable years.
4. Cash flow, working capital, and net worth are increased.
5. Funds in existing and diversified profit sharing plans may be released for reinvestment in company stock.
6. It provides a vehicle for the purchase of major blocks of stock in closely held companies.

Usually such a purchase by the company would be considered a redemption of shares by the IRS, thereby subjecting the selling stockholder to ordinary income taxes and eliminating the company's tax deduction. However, if the ESOP buys stock, the selling stockholder is taxed on a capital gains basis and the company's contributions to cover the cost of the stock purchase are tax deductible.

Sometimes companies make ESOP contributions in the form of stock and, in the process, recapture taxes already paid. For example, assume that a company has a

80

taxable income totaling $1 million over a 3-year period and breaks even in the fourth year.

By contributing $1-million worth of its stock to the ESOP, a tax-deductible outlay, the company creates a $1-million loss. This can be carried back to offset all the taxable income in the prior 3 years.

An ESOP can also be used to refinance corporate debt with pretax dollars. This is accomplished by having the ESOP borrow an amount equal to the debt and then using the borrowed cash to purchase company shares. In turn, the company pays off its debt with the cash received from the sale of the shares to ESOP and then commences making tax-deductible contributions to its ESOP, so that the latter can repay its borrowing.

OTHER FINANCING SOURCES

Short-Term Financing

Commercial banks have short-term loans that generally take the form of unsecured lines of credit designed for seasonal requirements. Generally, the bank requires proof of the borrower's ability to repay the loan from earnings, inventory reduction, etc. If management feels that it is possible to obtain local operators for their units fairly rapidly, then it may be feasible to employ these short-term funds for the accumulation of real estate sites and the subsequent construction and equipping of branches. To liquidate this temporary financing, this company could then arrange a blanket mortgage or a sale and lease-back with an institutional lender.

If the company is fortunate, it may have a "revolving credit" arrangement. This is a better situation because the funds are drawn only as required and, thus, interest is saved. Also, this type of loan does not appear on the financial statement as a "current liability."

Intermediate-Term Financing

This is characterized by its length. Generally, it runs 3 to 5 years. It may be amortized monthly or quarterly and is usually secured by some corporate asset having a value in excess of the principal amount of the loan.

The bank requires certain information as to the purpose of the loan and to the security offered. The bank will then indicate the interest rate, amortization requirement, and the prepayment schedule.

Next, the bank requires agreement to certain standards while the loan is outstanding, for example:

1. Maintenance of minimum capital
2. Limitation of dividends and stock acquisitions
3. Limitation on borrowing other than from the lender

4. Maintenance of assets free of liens
5. Limitation on loans to others
6. Limitation on guaranteeing obligation of others
7. Restrictions against acquisitions, mergers, or consolidation with other companies
8. Restrictions on sale or loss of borrower's assets
9. Agreement to provide bank with interim financial statements and annual audited statements

Long-Term Senior Financing

This generally has a maturity of 10 to 20 years or longer. Such financing may take the form of (1) lease arrangements or (2) unsecured term loans and mortgage loans. Sources for long-term financing include institutions, such as insurance companies and pension funds. Another source is the public sale of bonds.

Current Assets Financing

This type of financing is usually secured by liens on receivables and inventories. While not a current asset, equipment loans are similar in effect. Commercial finance companies are the source for such loans.

SBICs and Venture Capital Groups

These groups make loans which might be marginal for the banks, but in addition to the loan obligations, most of these venture organizations expect an equity bonus for making the loan. The mistake should not be made of regarding these sources as being available for start-up operations. The word "venture" is a misnomer. In reality they are secondary lenders for substantial interest rates plus equity bonuses.

Government Sources

Here there are almost innumerable possibilities, which are constantly increasing in response to special interests. So, when it is desired to explore this area, it should be done on a current basis by knowledgeable personnel. Nevertheless, a list of some of the standard government sources may be helpful and may apply under certain circumstances:

Commercial, Industrial, and Financial
Small Business Administration
Treasury Department
Federal Reserve System
Federal Home Loan Bank
Maritime Administration

Office of Economic Assistance (Department of Commerce)

Agricultural Loans
Farm Credit Administration
Rural Electrification Administration

Farmers Home Administration

Commodity Credit Corporation

Housing and Community Development

Office of Transportation

Community Facilities Administration

Public Housing Administration

Urban Renewal Administration

Federal Housing Administration

Veterans Administration

Natural Resources

Department of Interior

Bureau of Reclamation

National Marine Fisheries Society

Bureau of Indian Affairs

International Finance

Export-Import Bank (Washington, D.C.)

Agency for International Development

Public Financing

When you are thinking in terms of a company about to embark upon a Branchising program, certain public financing alternatives are possible. A few of these alternatives are the sale of a minority equity interest, acquisition of control of a company already public, merging with a public company, or being acquired by a public company. Another possibility to try is the public offering of new stock.

There are certain advantages for a company operating in the public sector rather than through private ownership:

1. Cash is made available for financing purposes.
2. Net worth is increased.
3. Borrowing position is improved.
4. Stock option plans become possible.
5. A public market facilitates acquisitions.
6. Liquidity is improved.
7. Better quality operators are attracted to the company's program.

If your company believes that its financial position should be bolstered before undertaking a Branchising program and expects to accomplish this by the sale of an equity interest, the following checklist will be required:

1. A 5-year, audited financial history
2. Details of any stock-option plan
3. Details of profit sharing or pension plan
4. Elimination of special "insider" benefits
5. History of management principals
6. Selection of investment banker, registrar, and transfer agents

A last word of caution is to be sure to obtain an investment banker of the highest reputation because this will be a long association and what is done will permanently affect the company.

Supportive Techniques

BACKUP NEEDS FOR THE BRANCHISEE

The average Branchisee—in acquiring a branch—needs and seeks a "mentor" from the home office. He wants to "lean" on its more experienced judgment and is responsive to its continuing advice and direction. In fact, failing to obtain this, he would feel deprived of the essential benefits of his association.

They require that the company deal with them in the same manner in which one bargains with labor unions: as equals in the business operation.

Branchisees do not wish to be dictated to. They expect the parent to "sell" them on policy or operating changes. They wish the company to be sincere and to take them into confidence.

Interestingly, Branchisees desire parent assistance for certain personal goals: They want (1) company-sponsored, self-improvement programs, (2) their managerial capacities improved, (3) higher profits, and (4) help in financial budgeting. They would even welcome company-generated correspondence and postgraduate courses on various subjects.

They also look to the parent to provide dramatic advertising programs of a scope which they, themselves, cannot afford.

Also, viewing the parent's image as having a direct bearing on their profits, they expect that the parent will maintain an unblemished public image.

Branchisors also have a strong desire to participate in "forward planning." They have confidence in their own expertise and desire the parent to put it to work as a means of improving overall profits.

A very important factor to the operator is the interchange of ideas and communication with the Branchisor; the atmosphere of a "corporate presence" greatly improves the operator's sense of confidence and hence his competitive stance.

They desire that the parent expand dynamically but not at the expense of previously assigned territories.

They also seek company support in assisting them to become recognized in their communities. Also, they seek monies beyond salaries and bonuses and seek that, upon their death, their families will retain a "vested interest" in the business which they helped to create.

SIX

The parent companies have some legitimate demands of the Branchisees, too. The company requires that the Branchisee put his "best effort" into the business, adopt company programs, consider himself as part of a larger whole, and advance the interests of the entire organization.

SUPERVISING THE PROGRAM

As the first step in achieving proper supervision, the company needs a specific, predesignated "supervisor" plus a "supervision program." An associate cannot be properly supervised if there are no set channels of communication. These channels must be planned and organized in a methodical and easy-to-implement fashion.

Hence every branch program must have the equivalent of a "branch coordinator" who will supervise operations. He also functions to receive all operator inquiries and problems which he distributes through the proper channels and ascertains that they are resolved.

The basic element of supervision is "communication." Communication can be established through the following means:

Supervision via Mail Contacts

If the Branchisee is "abandoned" in his territory and deprived of communication with the parent company, morale is lost and sales efficiency is impeded. It's extremely important that a system of correspondence and other contacts be established and regularly maintained. Such mail contacts include:

House Organs. They are generally four pages on 8½-by-11 paper that contains news and views of the company and of other branch managers. These include news and accomplishments of Branchisees, personal news, new sales and administrative ideas, and similar material.

"Flash Bulletins." They are generally one-sheet messages (mimeographed) that convey a special instructive or inspirational message of immediate value to the Branchisee.

Letters. A regular system of letters should come from the home office to the Branchisee. For fullest effectiveness and maximum impact, these letters should emanate from a number of sources, e.g., president, sales manager, operator coordinator, etc. These letters should be written in a "chatty," personalized vein, conveying a feeling that the Branchisee is of utmost importance to the company and is constantly being watched in his progress.

Self-Check Activity Forms. Many organizations provide managers with forms of this type which list contacts made each week and the results of such contacts (e.g., sales, call-backs, turndowns, etc.). Each week, a copy is sent to the attention of the sales manager at the home office. This gives the home office the ability to evaluate the Branchisee's activities in his area and to expose any possible weaknesses. At the end of each month, the sales manager prepares an "activities profile" on the branch that delineates weaknesses and strengths. It sets forth specific, constructive recommendations for improving the situation.

Supervision via Phone Contacts

The telephone constitutes a strong force for inspiring, motivating, instructing, and guiding the manager, keeping him contented and in a proper attitude. Properly used, it is most valuable in achieving improved sales results. Telephone contacts can be classified as follows:

Calls Preceded by Letter.   Many companies find it effective to arrange person-to-person "chats" with each associate at least once a month. This helps to build a valuable rapport with the associate and does much to expose and solve problems as well as gripes. A letter is written to the associate advising him of the date and time he will receive this phone call. This approach has many benefits: First, it spurs the associate to greater efforts and accomplishments in anticipation of this phone call (so that he can report maximum results). Second, it gives him a sense of the "pleasant anticipation" that something favorable is going to occur several days hence, giving the phone call the utmost morale value.

Spontaneous Phone Calls.   Unscheduled and unexpected phone calls of this nature—especially when they emanate from an unexpected source, e.g., the president of his organization—helps greatly in boosting the morale of the associate and increasing his pride of "belonging" to his organization. Contacts of this type can be merely personal, friendly "chat-type" calls, or they may refer to current business events of interest to the associate.

Conference Phone Calls.   This, too, has proved to be highly effective. Companies will set up a conference phone call covering five to twenty associates in a given region. A preceding letter will advise everyone of the date and time of the conference call. The stated objectives of such phone calls are to inform associates of some new, important development, i.e., to announce a contest, a new product or service, a new means of enhancing their sales and income, etc.

Telephone company rates are moderate for such conference calls, and the results are well worth this comparatively small expense.

Supervision via Home Office Personnel

Personal appearances by company executives, from the home office, at the operator's place of business are very important and assure maximum accomplishment. This is a "must" that helps supplement the mail and phone contact procedures. This, too, should be done on a regular, systematic, prescheduled basis.

Such "personal-type" visits should be made at different intervals by any or all of the following members of the company organization: sales manager, president or vice president, branch coordinator, and manager service supervisor. The effect of such visits should be as follows:

"Trouble-Shooting."   In this role, the company member seeks to ascertain problems that have impeded progress—or have caused recurring objections and complaints from his customers—and to help solve them.

Sales "Backup."   Here, the member helps associates overcome sales difficulties due to inadequacies in such factors as approach, presentation, closed meeting objections, etc.

Service "Backup."   This acts to (1) help associates solve service problems that may currently exist; (2) help him obtain a current big job through assisting in his installation and estimating problems; and (3) accompany operator to installations that have been "complained about" by customers to help smooth out these difficulties.

Supervision via Managers Helping Each Other

Organizations have found it highly effective to enlist the aid of "stronger" associates to assist "weaker" associates. Often associates may not be completely responsive to advice and assistance from the home office. They interpret such efforts as "theoretical" or "prejudiced" toward home office objectives to a greater extent than to "associate" requirements. Hence the assignment of a successful associate to help an unsuccessful associate is the kindred, common goal among associates. He respects and trusts the recommendations since each has similar goals. He responds to the theory that "You can't argue with success." Thus he will faithfully absorb and use this instruction to help improve his own operation.

Organizations accomplish such "associate help" programs through:

1. Setting up a "big brother" status among associates
2. Setting up "regional territory" operators with the regional manager being in supervision of member associates within his area
3. Arranging for associates in contiguous territories to help
4. Home office supervisors

Here is an in-depth look at these last two points:

Adjoining Territories.   Associates derive encouragement from the knowledge that they can "talk out" their problems with other associates in adjoining areas. This provides a sense of "belonging" to a large family and helps their attitude and pride toward their work. Many parent organizations arrange the mechanics for the "getting together" of adjoining territorial associates at scheduled intervals. One parent—in the closed-circuit television field—arranged a "working together" arrangement with his associates. He enlisted the technical strength of one associate (who was weak in sales) and the sales ability of another associate (who was weak in technical aspects) to help each other and to support each other's weaknesses.

Home Office Supervisors.   Such individuals become "roving ambassadors" of the parent organization assisting associates in their problems and, in addition, encouraging them in their endeavors. Their functions include (1) examining the operator's books and activity records to ascertain "what is wrong" and in what areas improvement can be made; (2) counseling the operator in sales or service problems; (3) achieving improved communication between the operator and home office; and (4) helping the operator in improving relations with his customers.

Summary

The effect of all the foregoing is to impress companies on the importance of the "continuing guidance" of their associates. To the extent that this is achieved, to a maximum degree, the company organization that has experienced failure in its programming generally is one that has lacked constructive "hold" over its associates. Its associates become so many detached, separated, semihostile units rather than satisfied, smoothly functioning, cohesive members of a large, closely knit "family."

Proper supervision of associates achieves the following:

1. Builds morale
2. Decentralizes home office functions
3. Enables regional control and "follow-up"
4. Achieves channels for constant "communication" between the company and the associate
5. Assures maximum morale and "nips in the bud" discontents and hostilities before they become ingrained
6. Acts to place associates in a "winning momentum" during the first 6 months of their operation, normally the critical period, during which time they can irretrievably fail if not properly and closely supervised and supported

SELF-INSPECTION CHECKLIST PROGRAMS

Figure 6-1 is a sample series of self-inspection forms used by various parent companies. These programs have proved effective in both controlling product or service quality and extending the original training (in effect, providing a postgraduate-training course).

It has been found, in many instances, that self-policing by the individual associates is more effective and certainly more economically viable than rigorous parent inspections. In addition, resentment is averted and a harmonious relationship is encouraged.

The philosophy behind these self-inspection forms is this: No victory is achieved by "catching" somebody doing wrong. The same, if not increased, results can be achieved by letting these persons "catch" themselves. You have thus preserved their dignity and status, rather than demeaning their self-esteem.

Name_____ Store no._____ Location_____ Date_____

	Store exterior	Yes	No
1	Sidewalk clean		
2	Sidewalk in good repair		
3	Window — glass clean		
4	Window — proper signs		
5	Window — proper size lights		
6	Window — lights operating		
7	Window — base below clean		
8	Sign clean		
9	Sign lighted		
10	Entrance clean		
11	Doors in good condition		
12	Awning clean		
13	Awning in good repair		
14	Building walls in good repair		
15	Building walls clean		
16	Grassy area neat		
17	Rear of store neat		
18	Trash containers good condition		
19	Trash containers in place		
20			
21			
22			

	Store interior — front	Yes	No
23	Floor clean		
24	Ceiling in good condition		
25	Walls in good condition		
26	Fixtures in good condition		
27	Lights proper size		
28	All lights working		
29	Lights clean		
30	Phone booth clean		
31	Directory in good condition. If not order new one.		
32	Weighing scales clean		
33	Weighing scales accurate		
34	Stamp machines operating		
35	Glass in cases clean		
36	Area behind counters clean		
37	Trash containers in place		
38			
39			
40			
41			
42			
43			
44			

Figure 6-1

Merchandise departments		a Stock clean		b Stock in order		c Stock priced		d Any out of date		e Shelves filled		f Compulsory display use		g Discontinued mdse.		h	
		Yes	No	Yes	No	Yes	No	Yes	No	Yes	No	Yes	No	Yes	No	Yes	No
45	Proprietary																
46	Toiletries																
47	Cosmetics																
48	Baby																
49	Sundries																
50	Ice cream																
51	Candy, gum																
52	Tobacco																
53	Housewares																
54	Hardware																
55	Pet supplies																
56	Greeting cards																
57	School supplies																
58	Magazines, books																
59	Convalescent																
60	Photo supplies																
61																	
62																	
63																	
64																	
65																	

Prescription department		Yes	No
66	Stock clean		
67	Stock in order		
68	Drawer mdse. in order		
69	Outdated – unsaleable mdse. pulled		
70	Scales and weights clean		
71	Prescriptions double – checked and signed		
72	Narcotic prescription canceled		
73	All restricted drugs dispensed by registered pharmacist		
74	Proper utensils on hand		
75	Utensils in proper condition		
76	Narcotic cabinet locked		
77	Prescription records in order		
78	Prescription files in order		
79	Sale of poisons recorded		
80	Sale of narcotics recorded		
81	Poison control emergency phone #		
82	Reference books in place		
83	Containers and bottles neat		
84	Containers and bottles in sufficient supply, right sizes		
85	Refrigerator in order		
86	Proper items under refrigeration		
87			
88			
89			

Storage and supplies in reserve		Yes	No
90	Mdse. stock neatly arranged		
91	Arranged by dept.		
92	Items of same category together in same place		
93	Trash containers in place		
94	Floor clean		
95	Packaging supplies neat		
96	Packaging supplies sufficient		
97	Supply of forms sufficient		
98	Cleaning supplies neat		
99	Cleaning supplies sufficient		
100	Reserve register tape rolls		
101	Lighting sufficient		
102			
103			
104			
105			
106			
107			
108			

Personnel		Yes	No
109	Neatly dressed		
110	Clean jackets		
111	Clean shaven, neat haircuts		
112	Clean hands, fingernails		
113	Good customer approach		
114	Courtesy		
115	Familiar with mdse.		
116	Lost sales recorded		
117	Know regular customer names		
118	Proper register procedure		
119	Proper change making		
120	Interest in work		
121	Smoking habits controlled		
122	Personal phone calls controlled		
123			
124			
125			
126			
127			
128			
129			

General		Yes	No
130	Bulletins and checklists posted		
131	Charge acct. procedure followed		
132	Fire extinguishers renewed and in proper places		
133	Register receipts legible		
134	Photo work (developing) kept orderly		
135	Photo work record kept		
136	Store licenses and certificates posted prominently		
137	Cigar humidor working and filled		
138	Air conditioning OK		
139	Wrapping, bagging material on hand in right places		
140	Displays and price signs clean		
141	Emergency phone numbers at hand		
142			
143			
144			
145			
146			
147			

Washroom		Yes	No
148	Floor clean		
149	Ceiling, walls clean		
150	Lighting sufficient		
151	Mirror clean		
152	Basin clean		
153	Toilet bowl clean		
154	Towels in place		
155	Soap sufficient		
156	Toilet paper and spare roll		
157	Waste receptacle		
158	Door lock in order		
159			
160			
161			
162			

INSTRUCTIONS: 1. When Used by Store Managers for Self-Inspection. Make notes of deficiencies on reverse side of this sheet. Identify each comment by line number corresponding to the item. Retain for your own use as a check on correction of deficiencies noted.

2. When Used by Field Supervisors. Sign and attach this form to field supervisor's inspection report form. It then becomes part of your report.

FIELD SUPERVISOR'S SIGNATURE_____

BRANCHING

SKY CHEFS' QUALITY CONTROL PROGRAM

As any restaurateur will attest, among the crucial factors that either impede or achieve repetitive patronage is the quality of the food, service, and general appearance of the restaurant. Insuring this quality through proper quality control is vital in achieving a consistently favorable quality image, in inducing return patronage, and in encouraging word-of-mouth advertising.

More and more operations are adopting both innovative and stronger quality control measures. One of the foremost innovators in this field is Sky Chefs, a subsidiary of American Airlines. Sky Chefs is one of the most extensive food purveyors in the country, servicing in-flight meals for some 36 airlines and providing a food service for thousands of travelers daily in its many airport restaurants.

A 25-point quality control standards program has been devised under the direction of Sky Chefs' A. C. Ferrari, President. The program requires observations in the following areas of performance,

Administration—Airline catering
Safety procedures
Delay performance
Meal components
Sanitation & housekeeping
Completeness of equipment
Automotive maintenance
Automotive appearance
AFEH appearance
Equipment washing machines
Refrigerator/Freezers
Conservation of customer equipment
Hot food transporters
On-time arrival

Food handling/Conformance to specifications
Galley temperatures
Administration—Public facilities
Waiter/Waitress
Host/Hostess
Cashier
Bartender
Cocktail waiter/waitress
Snack bar
Sanitation
Service kitchen
Facilities maintenance and cleaning
Retail shop

Performance is checked out by the management of each food unit. An error factor from 0–10%, depending on the category, is permitted. In the event that the error factor is greater, a Quality Control Action Form is filled out and dispatched to the Regional Vice President, along with an explanation of what measures have been taken to correct the errors.

As explained by Mr. Ferrari in the Sky Chefs' Quality Control Manual:

Sky Chefs' Quality Control Program is a positive action program which allows unit management to measure performance based on predetermined standards set by operations and staff personnel.

The purpose of the program is to provide local management with a tool to both measure and improve service to our customers.

In order for our Quality Control Program to be an effective tool, the following requirements must be met:

1. Observations are to be made by members of management, who must familiarize themselves with the instructions as outlined in the sections applicable to the areas being checked.
2. Catering Kitchen management shall conduct observations in Airline Catering categories and Public Facilities management shall conduct observations in Public Facility categories.
3. Observations must be made on a random basis at various times of the day so that all shifts are included.
4. Reporting must be accurate and accomplished on a systematic basis as set forth in the instructions.
5. Corrective action must be taken immediately on those areas found to be below standard.
6. Management on all levels must become totally involved with the program and view it as constructive and positive.

Mr. Ferrari goes on to say:

It is not the purpose of our quality control program to "police" unit management. It is rather an Awareness Program. As these standards are checked off and graded daily by the management, there is a growing awareness of the problem areas and corrective measures required—e.g., untidy waitress uniforms, an unclean spatula, and so on. Our main office evaluator appears at each unit, at unscheduled intervals, to recheck the "grades."

We consider the Quality Control Program so important that I personally review the statistics each month.

Mr. Ferrari states that this program serves the dual purpose of instilling both quality control and enhanced morale among personnel, achieving a sense of team effort. On the following pages are some of the forms that Sky Chefs uses to ensure proper quality control.*

Thus quality control, for restaurants and purveyors alike, is one of the most important factors in projecting a caring, quality management and operation. If you project an attractive appearance, an appealing decor, considerate and helpful personnel, interesting and unusual food preparations, and a quality operation, you have a good opportunity for gaining a large and loyal clientele.

*Used with permission of Sky Chefs, New York.

SKY CHEFS

Cafeteria—Observation Record

Unit _____
Month of _____

	1	2	3	4	5	6	7	8	9	10	11	12	13	14	15
													DINNER		
DATE/OBSERVER															
a Attendant Personality															
b Personal Appearance															
c Additional Sales Attempted															
d Appearance of Food And Steamtable															
e Clean Tables And Filled And Clean Condiments															
f Menu Board															
g Cash Handling															
h Tableware Available And Clean															
i General Neatness And Cleanliness															
Name or Initials of Individual Observed															
Record Entire Observation as Std (√) or Below Std (X)															
Comments															

No Observations Standard A _____

Total No Observations B _____

% Monthly Performance C _____

$A \div B = C$

Record C on Line B-7 of Form QSS

95

Food Handling Procedures/Conformance To Specifications

OBSERVATION NO.	1	2	3	4	5	6	7	8	9	10	11	12	13	14	15	16	17	18	19	20	21	22	23	24	25	26	27	28	29	30
1. Receiving Procedures Followed																														
2. Recipes & Specifications Followed																														
3. Food Handling Procedures Followed																														
4. Cooking Equipment Functioning																														
5. Useable Food Not Discarded																														
6. Over Portioning Controlled																														
7. Over Production Minimized																														
8. Proper Cleaning Habits Followed																														
9. Meals Prepared with Care																														
10. Security & Control Adequate																														
OBSERVATION STANDARD (✓) OR BELOW STANDARD (X)																														
OBSERVERS INITIALS																														

Indicate Observation as Standard (✓) or Below Standard (X) in the appropriate columns.

A. No. Observations Standard

B. Total Observations

C. % Monthly Performance A ÷ B = C

Record this figure on line A-14, Form QSS

QC-265 REV. 1-75

SKY CHEFS

AFEH Uniform Appearance Performance

Unit _____

Month of _____

DATE / OBSERVER	1	2	3	4	5	6	7	8	9	10	11	12	13	14	15	16	17	18	19	20	21	22	23	24	25	26	27	28	29	30
Shirt: Sky Chefs Specs A																														
Pants: Sky Chefs Specs B																														
Bump Cap: Specs With Logo Affixed C																														
Security Badge Visible D																														
Torn or Dirty Clothes Worn E																														
Haircut, Sideburns or Mustache per local Management F																														
Initials of Driver/Helper G																														
Record entire Obs. as Std. (✓) or Below Std. (X)																														

OBS. NO., ACTION TAKEN & DATE OF REVIEW

No. Observations Standard A. ☐

Total No. Observations B. ☐

% Monthly Performance C. ☐
A ÷ B = C

Record on
Line A-8 of
Form QSS

QC-259 REV 1-75

Revision Record

Place this record in the front of your manual. Immediately on receipt of revisions, insert and remove pages as required. Enter the date the revision is inserted. If revisions are not received in numerical order, request missing ones from American Airlines In-Plant Printing, LGA.

If By Board Mail: AA In-Plant Printing
LGA

If by U.S. Mail: In-Plant Printing
American Airlines, Inc.
LaGuardia Airport Station
Flushing, New York 11371

REV. NO.	DATE INSERTED	REV. NO.	DATE INSERTED	REV. NO.	DATE INSERTED	REV. NO.	DATE INSERTED
1		26		51		76	
2		27		52		77	
3		28		53		78	
4		29		54		79	
5		30		55		80	
6		31		56		81	
7		32		57		82	
8		33		58		83	
9		34		59		84	
10		35		60		85	
11		36		61		86	
12		37		62		87	
13		38		63		88	
14		39		64		89	
15		40		65		90	
16		41		66		91	
17		42		67		92	
18		43		68		93	
19		44		69		94	
20		45		70		95	
21		46		71		96	
22		47		72		97	
23		48		73		98	
24		49		74		99	
25		50		75		100	

BRANCHISING

SKYCHEFS

Comparative Quality Statistics Summary Form

UNIT _____

AIRLINE CATERING BACK OF THE HOUSE	STD	1975												1976											
		JAN	FEB	MAR	APR	MAY	JUN	JUL	AUG	SEP	OCT	NOV	DEC	JAN	FEB	MAR	APR	MAY	JUN	JUL	AUG	SEP	OCT	NOV	DEC
A-1 Safety Procedures	100																								
A-2 Delay Performance	99.8																								
A-3 Meal Components	93																								
A-4 Sanitation/Housekeeping	90																								
A-5 Completeness of Equip.	93																								
A-6 Auto Maintenance	90																								
A-7 Auto Appearance	90																								
A-8 AFEH Appearance	93																								
A-9 Equip. Wash. Machines	93																								
A-10 Refrigerators/Freezers	93																								
A-11 Cons. of Cust. Equip.	93																								
A-12 Hot Food Transporters	93																								
A-13 On Time Arrival	93																								
A-14 Food Handling/Specs.	97																								

FRONT OF THE HOUSE	STD	1975												1976											
		JAN	FEB	MAR	APR	MAY	JUN	JUL	AUG	SEP	OCT	NOV	DEC	JAN	FEB	MAR	APR	MAY	JUN	JUL	AUG	SEP	OCT	NOV	DEC
B-1 Waitress/Waiter	90																								
B-2 Hostess	90																								
B-3 Cashier	90																								
B-4 Bartender	90																								
B-5 Cocktail Waitress	90																								
B-6 Snack Bar	90																								
B-7 Cafeteria	90																								
B-8 Service Kitchen	90																								
B-9 Maintenance & Cleaning	93																								
B-10 Retail Shops	90																								

Quality Control Manual

Section 1

Page 1

May 1-76

ADMINISTRATION OF
QUALITY CONTROL PROGRAM

Sky Chefs Quality Control Program is a positive action program which allows unit management to measure their unit's performance based on pre-determined standards set by operations and staff personnel. In Airline Catering locations, the program includes 15 categories and in Public Facility locations, 10 categories. In those dual facility locations, the program consists of 25 categories, 15 airline catering and 10 public facility. Administrative instructions for airline catering locations precedes the Airline Catering section (A) of this manual and those for Public Facility locations precedes the Public Facility section (B).

The purpose of the program is to provide local management with a tool to both measure and improve service to our customers.

In order for our Quality Control Program to be an effective tool, the following requirements must be met:

1. Observations are to be made by members of management, who must familiarize themselves with the instructions as outlined in the sections applicable to the areas being checked.

2. Catering Kitchen management shall conduct observations in Airline Catering categories and Public Facilities management shall conduct observations in Public Facility categories.

3. Observations must be made on a random basis at various times of the day so that all shifts are included.

4. Reporting must be accurate and accomplished on a systematic basis as set forth in the instructions.

5. Corrective action must be taken immediately on those areas found to be below standard.

6. Management on all levels must become totally involved with the program and view it as constructive and positive.

ADMINISTRATION/UNIT MANAGEMENT

Upon completion of each individual observation, the results (Standard (✓) or Below Standard (X)) are to be entered in the applicable block on the appropriate form.

At the end of each month, the percentage scores for each area/item are

Quality Control Manual

to be computed and recorded on the Sky Chefs Quality Statistics
Summary Form (QC-248). A copy of this form will be forwarded to
the respective Regional/City Vice President, and Manager - Safety
and Sanitation - NYCQ, no later than the 10th day of the following
month. Performances and/or areas rated as Below Standard require
detailed written explanation as to why Standard was not attained
and what follow-up corrective action was taken or is planned. The
Quality Control Action Form (QC-266) shall be used for this summary and separate forms are to be used for Airline Catering
items/areas and Public Facility items/areas, and these reports
must accompany the QC-248.

Each unit will be required to maintain locally a Comparative Quality
Control Statistics Summary Form (QC-249) for purposes of determining
trends.

ADMINISTRATION/CORPORATE OFFICE

Upon receipt of unit reports, the Manager - Safety and Sanitation will:

1. Prepare a system Quality Statistics Summary Form, circling all
    Below Standard areas. When all unit figures have been reported,
    a copy of system performance will be forwarded to the President,
    his staff and Regional/City Vice Presidents.

2. Forward Public Facility statistics and Action Forms to the Customer
    Services Department.

3. Prepare specifically tailored airline catering Quality Statistics
    Summaries, recapping performance on various airline accounts.

RESPONSIBILITY/UNIT MANAGEMENT

Every General Manager/City Vice President is responsible for compliance
by his unit with the requirements of the company Quality Control Program.
Each General Manager/City Vice President must make certain that the
figures are accurate and ensure that corrective action is taken immediately
after discrepancies are noted. He is required to personally participate
in the program to assure that the unit is performing at the highest
quality level. Should an area be "Below Standard" he is required to forward to the respective Regional Vice President an explanation on the
Quality Control Action Form with a copy to Manager - Safety and Sanitation, NYCQ along with Form QC-248.

SUPPORTIVE TECHNIQUES   101

Recruitment

One of the most important aspects of the Branchising program is recruitment. By this, we mean contacting and acquiring qualified associates for your program at a predesignated pace. The success or failure of a program can be based on the quality of your associates and the effectiveness of your communications and supervisory procedures.

It is usually best to recruit Branchisees in "clusters," that is, from areas that are adjacent to each other. The initial effort should be in clustered areas that are accessible to the parent home office. Thereafter, other clustered areas can be approached. This provides the opportunity to handle personnel and other requirements on an economical and efficient basis, plus the collateral economic advantage gained by group advertising.

Generally speaking, the following steps are required for effective recruitment:

1. Preliminary preparation of qualification criteria for associates. This must be highly detailed, so that it provides a thorough and realistic profile of the type of individual that you deem to be an acceptable associate.
2. Determination of the areas to be allotted. This should be based on predeveloped criteria for site selection, to assure that each branch location has virtually guaranteed earnings potential. (See Chapter 13.)
3. Assessment of media to be used for prospecting for qualified associates. A budget should be projected based on estimated media costs per "sold" associate.
4. Preparation of systems, procedures, and flow and control forms to provide a careful record of prospects, media sources, and results of personal contacts. Figures 7-1 to 7-5 are sample flow and control forms.

QUALIFICATION CRITERIA FOR ASSOCIATES

The following outline lists suggested criteria for selecting a Branchisee:

1. Status and Education
    a. Married
    b. Age 26–60

SEVEN

c. Homeowner with substantial fixed personal overhead

d. College degree or solid business experience

2. Financial Background

a. History of income from $18,000–$30,000 a year

b. Able to make Branchise investment from own funds or easily obtainable source

c. Able to finance leasehold improvements, inventory, and working capital requirements—(some company assistance may be offered here if individual is qualified)

3. Skills

a. Ability to communicate verbally

b. Sensitive to the reactions and desires of prospects

c. Flexibility in dealing with all kinds of people

d. Concept of business and money

4. Demeanor

a. Acceptable physical appearance

b. Acceptable dress and cleanliness

c. Nonaggressive manner

POSSIBLE MEDIA FOR LOCATING BRANCHISE PROSPECTS

Investors can be sought through print advertising. *The Wall Street Journal* and the Sunday *New York Times,* for example, are both recognized as leading marketplaces for locating investors. Classified and display advertising in local newspapers in selected markets may also prove productive. Your announcement could be listed under "Business Opportunities" in the financial pages. In addition, advertisements in trade publications can be valuable, since the subject matter is aimed at the type of person you seek as a Branchisee.

The names of prospective investors can also be obtained through local referrals made by, for example, bank presidents, the chamber of commerce, business brokers, real estate brokers, local business and professional groups, local newspaper editors, contractors, architects, builders, etc.

Finally, investors can be sought by conducting seminars. An "Own Your Own Business" seminar often attracts from 100 to 300 prospective investors.

SYSTEMS, PROCEDURES, AND FORMS

A "system" should be established for maintaining prospect leads, to help:

1. Simplify the search for records and correspondence

2. Provide cross-reference files allowing various means of information, classification, and retrieval

3. Set up means of "logging-in" inquiries which will provide evaluation data for equating advertising dollars spent in various media
4. Establish "follow-up" procedures
5. Provide means of recording phone calls, checking salesperson's activities, and checking the progress of prospects

Filing System

In addition to the numerical master file, which will carry the original inquiry, all correspondence, and forms, you will need two "cross-files" and a "follow-up" file system.

The cross-files will consist of the following:

1. Prospects filed alphabetically (on pink carbon copy of letter)
2. Prospects filed by state with cities filed alphabetically within state sections (on blue carbon copy of letter)

The follow-up file can be either an accordian, multisectioned envelope or a hanging file. For follow-up purposes, a third copy of the inner-address portion of the letter will be made on a specially prepared form. This form will be kept in the master file except when it is removed and placed into the follow-up file. It will have space to enter information, such as first phone contact, interview date, remarks, and follow-up remarks. (See Figure 7-1.)

Reference Numbers

Each inquiry as it is "logged" is given a "reference number." This number performs several functions: By providing a numerical sequence to the files, it makes retrieval faster and filing more accurate and dependable. Also, by incorporating a key number system, the reference number can instantly identify media sources and date of placement.

In order to perform these functions the following system is recommended:

Letter indicates inquiry source	First two digits indicate month of ad	Second two digits indicate date of ad	Fifth digit indicates last digit of year	Digits after hyphen indicate order of receipt
W	**08**	**06**	**9**	**100**
(Wall Street Journal)	(August)	(6)	(1979)	(One hundredth inquiry received)

LEAD FOLLOW UP CONTROL
FRANCHISE SALES DIVISION

| SOURCE CODE |
| REF. |
| DATE RECEIVED AT HOME OFFICE |
| SOURCE OF LEAD |

PROSPECT'S NAME _____

ADDRESS _____

CITY _____ ZONE _____ STATE _____ PHONE _____

| REQUIRED TIMING | √ | **PART 1—FOR USE AT HOME OFFICE** |

| Immediate | LOGGED IN FRANCHISE EVALUATION BOOK. RECEIPT DATE STAMPED ON INQUIRY. | √ |

| | O.K. FOR FURTHER PROCESSING | REJECTED |

| Within 48 Hours | FIRST RESPONSE PACKAGE MAILED. Date: ☐ New Construction ☐ Existing Motel ☐ Regional Reply Envelope Enclosed | BY: .... REASON: .... |

DISTRIBUTION

☐ 1 — 1st copy of Reply letter, original Inquiry, and original of this form to Master File in Numerical Sequence.

☐ 2 — 2nd copy of Reply letter, copy of Inquiry, 1st copy of this form to Regional Office at: City _____ Date:

☐ 3 — 3rd copy of Reply letter to City-State File.

☐ 4 — 4th copy of Reply letter to Alphabetical File.

Rejection letter mailed. Date:
This form with copies of Inquiry and Reply to REJECT FILE.

| √ | **PART 2—FOR USE AT REGIONAL OFFICE** |

| DATE RECEIVED AT REGIONAL OFFICE | NAME OF SALESMAN | DATE ASSIGNED | ☐ COPY OF REPLY LETTER TO ALPHABETICAL FILE |

| | INITIAL PHONE CONTACT | √ | PHONE CALL RESULTS |

Immediate	If Get-Acquainted Form Received		DATE	TIME
10 Days after Response Date	If Get-Acquainted Form NOT Received	Appointment Mode:	LOCATION
	PHONE DATE	DISPOSITION		NUMBER OF PEOPLE TO ATTEND
				ACCOMMODATION RESERVATIONS to be made, if necessary for: _____ people
				DISQUALIFIED. Reason:
	QUALIFIED. AMOUNT TO INVEST: $
	READY TO MOVE AHEAD. WHEN:		UNABLE TO REACH. Reason:
	DOESN'T HAVE SITE. HAS SITE AT:

| | **FOLLOW UP ACTION** |

Within 24 Hrs. of Phone Call resulting in Appointment	CONFIRMATION OF APPT. LETTER MAILED. Date: ☐ Letter #101 if appointment is at QUALITY OFFICE. ☐ Letter #102 if appointment is in FIELD.	CAN'T-REACH-BY-PHONE LETTER MAILED. Date: ☐ Letter #105 if Get-Acquainted form has been received. ☐ Letter #106 if Get-Acquainted form has NOT been received.
72 Hours prior to Appointment	FOLLOW-UP CONFIRMATION TELEGRAM SENT. Date: ☐ #103 if appointment is at QUALITY OFFICE. ☐ #104 if appointment is in FIELD.	ACCOMMODATION RESERVATION FOR PROSPECT MADE if appointment is to be at Quality Office.	DATE MADE
		FILE RETURNED TO HOME OFFICE if unable to contact by phone or letter — 4 weeks after lead was received.	DATE RETURNED

PRESENTATION MADE Date: ____ PARTIES ATTENDING: { .... }

CLOSING: ☐ AGREEMENT SIGNED | CHECK RECEIVED $ | ☐ CREDIT FORM FILLED OUT | ☐ PRELIMINARY SITE INSPECTION MADE BY: | DATE MADE

REMARKS:

IF SUCCESSFUL SALE OF FRANCHISE, COMPLETED FILE RETURNED TO HOME OFFICE, WITH: ☐ Franchise agreement ☐ Check ☐ Site Report ☐ Credit Form ☐ Map ☐ Corporate Resolutions | DATE MAILED: | IF UNSUCCESSFUL, FILE RETURNED TO HOME OFFICE. | DATE MAILED: | SALESMAN'S SIGNATURE:

| **PART 3—FOR USE AT HOME OFFICE** |

FINANCIAL REVIEW	STAFF COMMITTEE	☐ 15 Mile Notice	BOARD OF DIRECTORS	FEASIBILITY REPORT	AGREEMENT ACCEPTED	NOTICES SENT:
☐ Rejected ☐ Accepted	☐ Rejected ☐ Accepted	Date Sent	Date Referred	Date Ordered		Date
By:	By:		☐ Conditional Acceptance ☐ Rejected	Source	Date:	☐ Acceptance ☐ Rejection
Date:	Date:		Date:	☐ Satisfactory ☐ Unsatisfactory	By:	☐ To Licensee ☐ To Salesman

REMARKS: _____

| DISPOSITION OF FILE |
| ☐ To Operations |
| ☐ Other: _____ |
| DATE: |

Figure 7-1

In other words, the first inquiry received from the ad run on August 6, 1979, bears the reference number W–08079–1. The twentieth answer received is W-08079-20. The last digits are continuous from one ad to the next. This gives us a numerical sequence and identification for all inquiries. These last digits are the numerical sequence for the master file.

Recommended Materials

There are two means of conveniently handling the problem of making the simultaneous carbon copies:

1. Carbon interleaved snap-apart sets (three part or four part sets; the third and fourth parts being partially carbonized and having printed forms)
2. NCR (no carbon required) paper

Either or both should be available from local supply sources.

System for Recording and Evaluating Results of Advertising

A looseleaf book will be kept with a separate page (or pages) for each ad. The page will have enough space for a proof of the actual ad to be pasted on. There will also be space to record information. (See Figure 7-2.)

Box No. _____

Date of ad _____

Publication _____

Ref. No. prefix _____

Size _____

(Attach ad here)   Per line rate $ _____

Total cost $ _____

No. of inquiries _____

Cost per inquiry $ _____

No. of interviews _____

Cost per interview $ _____

No. of branches sold _____

Cost per branchise sold $ _____

	Date Rec'd	Ref. No.	Last Name	First Name	City	State	Phone Date	Interview Date
1								
2								
3								
4								
5								
6								
7								
8								
9								
10								
11								
12								

Figure 7-2

Immediately below the space reserved for attaching the ad proof and recording the above information would be space for "logging" inquiries as they arrive.

The printing should be with black ink on twenty-pound, #4 sulphate bond (8½-by-11 white paper), which is perforated for a three-hole binder. Use a good-quality looseleaf binder that is standard size and has opening and closing boosters and metal-hinged covers.

Record Sheets: Phone Calls

There are two important considerations in designing an effective record system for phone calls. First, it is necessary to record calls day by day and in the sequence made. Second, it is necessary to include a record of each phone conversation in the prospect's master file.

For this purpose a form with a two-part carbon is envisioned in which the first part is to be kept bound in a book as a permanent, day-by-day record and the second part is sectionally perforated so that each call can be separated from the others and placed with the prospect's master file. (See Figure 7-3.)

Sales Activity Sheets

These can be handled very similarly to the record sheets for phone calls with the exception that an extra copy should be made; one copy is for headquarters, one for the salesperson's file, and the perforated copy for the master file. These should be used to record all personal sales contacts whether they are "field calls" or "office interviews." It is especially important that the names of all parties at each meeting be recorded. (See Figures 7-4 and 7-5.)

EXAMPLE OF BRANCHISING SALES PROCEDURES

The following is a chronology of the procedures used by one Branchisor:

Upon receipt of an inquiry by a prospective Branchisee, a master card is typed for the file, to enable referral at a future date.

A form letter with an individually typed heading is then mailed out. Accompanying the letter is a prospectus, including cash investment data, and an application form to be completed and returned.

On receipt of the filled-out inquiry form, the Branchisor sends a letter that sets up an interview appointment. The Branchisee pays his own traveling expenses for an appointment at company offices.

At the interview, the main purpose is to assess the capabilities of the potential Branchisee by subjective criteria and not to endeavor to "sell" him a Branchise. You want to exchange information. The Branchisee should be aware of the negative aspects of the business as well as the positive ones.

Offer a tour of home office facilities and people. Also, visit an operation to answer

PHONE CALL RECORD

USE BALL POINT PEN
DETACH PERFORATED MESSAGES AND PLACE IN PROSPECTS MASTER FILE

PHONE CALL RECORD	DATE	TIME
PROSPECT'S NAME		
REF. NO.		
PHONE NO. AND CITY		☐ INCOMING

SIGNATURE	CALLED FROM ☐ OFFICE ☐ HOME OTHER

PHONE CALL RECORD	DATE	TIME
PROSPECT'S NAME		
REF. NO.		
PHONE NO. AND CITY		☐ INCOMING

SIGNATURE	CALLED FROM ☐ OFFICE ☐ HOME OTHER

PHONE CALL RECORD	DATE	TIME
PROSPECT'S NAME		
REF. NO.		
PHONE NO. AND CITY		☐ INCOMING

SIGNATURE	CALLED FROM ☐ OFFICE ☐ HOME OTHER

PHONE CALL RECORD

In duplicate

Top sheet--perforated message detached and placed idn prospect file

Dup. sheet not perf. Stays in employee's or departmental record book

PHONE CALL RECORD	DATE	TIME
PROSPECT'S NAME		
REF. NO.		
PHONE NO. AND CITY		☐ INCOMING

SIGNATURE	CALLED FROM ☐ OFFICE ☐ HOME OTHER

PHONE CALL RECORD	DATE	TIME
PROSPECT'S NAME		
REF. NO.		
PHONE NO. AND CITY		☐ INCOMING

SIGNATURE	CALLED FROM ☐ OFFICE ☐ HOME OTHER

PHONE CALL RECORD	DATE	TIME
PROSPECT'S NAME		
REF. NO.		
PHONE NO. AND CITY		☐ INCOMING

SIGNATURE	CALLED FROM ☐ OFFICE ☐ HOME OTHER

Figure 7-3

PERSONAL CONTACT RECORD

USE BALL POINT PEN

DISPOSITION OF PERFORATED SECTIONS: 1. TOP SHEET TO PROSPECT'S MASTER FILE 2. SECOND SHEET TO HEADQUARTERS
ENTIRE THIRD SHEET TO BE RETAINED IN EMPLOYEE'S OR SALESMAN'S RECORD BOOK

PERSONAL CONTACT RECORD

REF. NO.   DATE   TIME

PROSPECT'S NAME

WHERE ☐ FIELD ☐ OFFICE OTHER:

RESULTS

SIGNATURE

PERSONAL CONTACT RECORD

REF. NO.   DATE   TIME

PROSPECT'S NAME

WHERE ☐ FIELD ☐ OFFICE OTHER:

RESULTS

SIGNATURE

PERSONAL CONTACT RECORD

REF. NO.   DATE   TIME

PROSPECT'S NAME

WHERE ☐ FIELD ☐ OFFICE OTHER:

RESULTS

SIGNATURE

PERSONAL CONTACT RECORD

REF. NO.   DATE   TIME

PROSPECT'S NAME

WHERE ☐ FIELD ☐ OFFICE OTHER:

RESULTS

SIGNATURE

Figure 7-4

BRANCHISING

DATE	NAME AND ADDRESS OF PROSPECT	ORIGIN OF LEAD				HOW CONTACT WAS MADE			MEETING HELD OR PLANNED (Date)	WHERE	RESULT			REMARK
		Personal solicitation	Home office ad reply	Local ad reply	Other	Phone	Letter	In person			No	Future call-back date	Branch, sold	

SALESPERSON _____ OFFICE _____
CONDENSED MONTHLY SUMMARY OF   SALES ACTIVITY PERIOD _____

Figure 7-5

on-the-spot questions. At the end of the meeting (which normally lasts 1½ to 2½ hours), ask the prospect if he would like further data. If so and you are satisfied with him, provide him with the Branchise agreement (two copies), a financial information sheet, a psychological test, and an application form. Ask him to fill it out at home. After receiving advice from his attorney or accountant, he should submit the signed agreement with a designated deposit. A response letter is mailed out when the check is received, indicating it will take several weeks to approve his application. During this time his financial sheet, his application form, his psychological test, and his credit worthiness are analyzed. Perhaps a credit check should also be conducted.

On your approval of this Branchisee, notification is sent to him and a signed copy of the Branchise agreement is forwarded. If he is not approved, a letter of explanation enclosing his check is sent to him.

Branchise agreements, forms, tests, literature, etc., are frequently modified. However, the basic "substance" of the agreement should remain unchanged.

After the Branchisee leaves the interview, a special form is completed containing relevant information. This is kept in a special file or placed in the Branchise agreement jacket with all his completed forms. A history, which will prove invaluable at some future date, is thus built up pertinent to the Branchisee.

Once the Branchisee has, with the payment of his fee, joined the organization, a series of properly spaced letters outlining activities on his behalf by the different departments in the company are sent. If there appears to be some delay in getting him into business, a program of activities should be initiated to maintain his interest during the wait.

All the correspondence with the Branchisee is recorded on a special form. All the appropriate department heads are notified concerning this prospective Branchisee.

Once the site has been located, the Branchisee is notified and shown it for his approval and is given various justifications for the selected site. If he approves the site, he will sign a lease or sublease, subject to variances, and pay the security deposit.

When construction starts (or 2 months prior to its completion), the Branchisee will be invited in for training. When he arrives for training or when unit construction starts, he will be asked to sign an equipment order indicating all the items and the appropriate cost. The Branchisee must have the prescribed down payment, and it is his obligation to pay for or finance the remaining monies when the equipment is installed.

The financing aspects must be completed within 2 to 3 weeks; therefore, the company must have access to outside finance companies that will handle the financing promptly if the Branchisee doesn't have his own sources. Of course, the company could consider doing its own financing with a separate leasing or financing subsidiary. There are many good and valid reasons for doing this in-company.

After in-house schooling, the Branchisee returns to complete the preopening program and to hire employees and managers. Supervisors are available to help him during this period and to install equipment or to help with installation. On the Saturday or Sunday before opening, which would be on a Monday, the supervisor returns to handle the training class. The supervisor stays all week with the Branchisee—training and retraining the "students." He ascertains that the Branchise knows how to complete and analyze all operational and accounting forms, and before he leaves, the supervisor prepares a supervisor's report.

The Branchisee will submit monthly royalty payments, on a special form, monthly P&L statements, yearly audited statements with his balance sheet, certain daily operational forms (sent weekly), and other forms. An operations analyst will constantly check these forms and reports to be able to notify the Branchisees—either directly or through supervisors—of possible areas for improvement. Improvement must be forthcoming. All verbal and written correspondence with the Branchisee should be kept in a special Branchisee file for reference and historical patterns. Record-keeping systems become important and occupy a great deal of space.

The continuing relationship with the Branchisee includes the numerous special forms for particular circumstances; the additional controls and reports; the added and special services that are offered the Branchisee; the planned feeding of information and changes to the Branchisee; the correction of problems; the relationship of the supervisor to the home office and Branchisee; the continuing development of the branchise system and the operations; the continuing development and sophistication of the home office organization; the need to anticipate Branchisee unrest and how to deal with it; seminars, meetings, and conventions; and the implementation of advertising programs on a local, regional, and national basis.

This, plus all the functions performed by the different departments in the company that relate to the Branchisee, helps to assure a successful Branchisee and a healthy Branchisor-Branchisee relationship.

SUMMATION OF BRANCHISING PROCEDURES

1. The Branchise application and financial application are approved, and the Branchisee fee is paid.
2. The site is selected by the Branchisor, and approval of the site is signed by the applicant.
3. The lease is signed and the lease deposit is paid.
4. Before construction begins, the balance of the equipment lease deposit and the land lease deposit are required.
5. Evidence of adequate working capital must be demonstrated to the company.
6. The aforesaid should be "documented" with a series of procedural letters of agreement to be prepared for every step.
7. Consideration may be given to all rents becoming due at one time in the event of forfeiture by Branchisee.
8. While the unit is under construction, the Branchisee is notified to come for training.

Training

At the operator's level, the essence of a successful Branch expansion program and the base for all future attitudes (company loyalty and the controlled drive and implementation of the branch program) are implanted in the weeks that the operator is under the direction of the home office for the initial training. It is during this short period of time that the groundwork for all future relationships is "cemented." It is imperative that the time spent with the operator during his training achieves the desired results.

The operator must be convinced that running his business is his opportunity to take his place in the business community as an astute and successful businessperson, rendering a needed service to his community while making a profit for himself.

Attitudes leading to a success pattern are infused, not taught, during the training period, and the selection of a training manager must be a careful and thoughtful process. He must be a person who engenders confidence, rapport, respect, and a desire to emulate. The training manager must be thoroughly versed in all operational aspects of the business, including personnel management, community relations, public relations, bookkeeping, housekeeping, inventory control, and customer service.

We must assume, in this program as in any other program, that our operator has no business background; therefore, part of the training period must be devoted to the basic principles of business management, profit motives, and cost control.

EXAMPLE OF TRAINING CURRICULUM

Here is a sample training curriculum that a restaurant chain would use in the development of its Branchisees. Notice the wide range of courses and how every aspect of the business is covered.

Basic business facts

How to read and analyze your balance sheet

How to prepare and analyze your P&L statement

Costs—direct and indirect

Functions of the cash register including sales slips, disbursements in cash, cash register tapes, and how to read them

How to set up your register in the morning

How to close out your register in the evening

Bank deposit slips—how to fill them out

Night deposits at the bank

How to disburse cash when needed for deliveries, etc.

Petty cash—function

EIGHT

Petty cash vouchers—two ways to use them

Register control—cash versus sales checks

Personnel selection, training and management

Food preparation methods

Mixing the beverage formulas

Serving

Merchandising, advertising, and sales promotion

Ordering procedures, from home office

Ordering procedures, from local suppliers

Food storage methods

Inventory control

Sanitary controls

Bookkeeping procedures

Customer relations

Basic facts, benefits, and whys about the restaurant business, including procedures, attributes, and criteria

Facts about the parent company and its origin and growth

The people behind the company—brief descriptions of whom to contact relative to various functions and problems

Getting established—preopening procedures

Getting established—opening and post-opening procedures (including the grand opening)

Ordering equipment, supervising construction

Professional and personal services needed; also licenses and permits.

Personnel recruitment and training

Kitchen operation

Establishing job specifications of various personnel

Food portion control

Advertising and promotions

Knowing the "arithmetic" of your business

   Need for profitability

   Knowing your operating ratios

   Knowing your break-even point

Record-keeping system

  How to use it

  Making up deposit slips

Maintaining communications with the home office

Your lease—what it means and how to live with it

Labor laws and practices

Workers' compensation

Social Security

City, state, federal, and withholding taxes

Insurance—why and how much

Contingent liabilities

Profit

Motivation of employees

Psychologically and economically, it is best that the home office training be done in groups of at least three associates. The economic advantages are obvious. From an educational standpoint, it is better to work with a group because it engenders an interplay of ideas and a feeling of group vitality.

In-Store Training

Following the home office training, the operator and his staff will receive additional "in-store" training prior to his grand opening. Initially, the branch director will handle all phases of both home office and field training. As the operations grow, the training duties will be assumed by other executives appointed for this purpose.

Field Representative

The parent company must stand ready to send a qualified representative to the operator and to literally "hold his hand" as he experiences the first few months of business. This representative must be able to retrace all the steps of the training program in the field and reinspire him with the same initial drive and spirit.

During the first critical few months, each operator should receive at least one telephone call per week from the parent company and/or a visit from the field representative to bolster his morale and to reaffirm his initial resolve. It is during this period that the foundation of a lasting, profitable relationship is established. The parent company must not let this opportunity slip away, for it is at this time that the retention of a loyal, productive associate for many years to come can be assured by offering wisdom, kindness, sympathy, and direct sales help.

Additional refresher training may be established at a later date, as needed.

District and Regional Seminars

The long-range program should provide for district and regional seminars to be part of the continuous training of the Branchisees. These clinics give both the company and the operator an opportunity to discuss common problems, methods of operation, and promotional programs. Clinics are utilized to establish rapport between company and branch manager. Here, operators are given the opportunity to meet each other and to learn from each other. Many unique and successful methods of operation, tried and proven by branch managers, are brought to the fore during such seminars and clinics. Giving the operator an opportunity to "talk shop" with his fellow managers proves a valuable experience for all concerned. Properly handled and controlled, the seminars and clinics have a motivational value that is a valuable asset to the program.

The following is the four-week training program for new store owners given by the Ben Franklin Stores.

Ben Franklin
Four-Week New Store
Owner
Training Schedule*

Most Ben Franklin Franchisees have retailing experience and, in fact, the greatest majority of them have variety store background. More than one half of new Ben Franklin Franchisees are former Chain Store Managers and, therefore, they genuinely have a rich background in variety store retailing—all we need to teach them is the Ben Franklin Program and Systems.

To accomplish this, each new store owner attends a four-week training session at one of approximately 20 training stores around the country. These stores are owned and operated by individual franchisees and they voluntarily give their time to train new owners under actual every day operating conditions. Training costs are included in the franchisee's initial investment for his new store.

In addition to the following program for in-store training, all new franchisees also spend three days in any one of eight of our Regional Offices for indoctrination.

Place a check in the right-hand column when the scheduled item is completed and understood.

FIRST WEEK—CHECKING, ORDERING AND RECEIVING PROCEDURES

First Day—Welcome and Introduction to all store personnel. Pull the organization together for a brief meeting, emphasizing that it is an honor to have Mr. _____ with them for four weeks, an honor to be the store selected to serve as the trainee store for assisting Mr. _____ to do a better job in his new store.

At this time briefly explain the four-week training program.

Spend time reviewing in-store activity on sales floor and general operation of the store with tour of each department observing merchandise assortment. _____

*Used with permission of Thad Gruchot, Vice President, Ben Franklin Stores, Des Plaines, Ill., 1979.

(*New* owner's daily work schedule should be the same as the owner in whose store he is training.)

Review of all Check List books. _____

At the end of each day the new owner should make a list of things he may not have completely understood that day. The next day should begin with a brief review for clarification.

Second Day—Stockroom Spend a full day receiving/checking freight. (This should be on a day when Ben Franklin warehouse order is received.) _____

Indoctrination of freight book and its relationship to the operation. Enter the day's shipments. _____

Proper pricing procedure, marking merchandise, dating style goods, advantages of using new pre-printed price labels. _____

Tour of stockroom, covering proper layout, stock alignment. _____

Protection of merchandise against *soilage* and *pilferage, security, claim area, supplies, fixtures, lay-aways, seasonal carryover.* _____

(All these key points will be covered individually over the next four-week period.)

Third and Fourth Days—Merchandising Complete review of Check List books, on the sales floor, with the sales person in each department; study of layouts and Check List diagrams, association of Key Items to display; review of drop-list items, SMS and new items added. _____

Review of Basic Factory and Seasonal Listings. _____

It is important here to assign a specific person to handle each area during these two (2) days.

Fifth and Sixth Days Check and order entire departments using E.O.S. (On store's transmitting day, actually handle transmitting procedure of an order. It is important here to assign a specific person to handle this area.) _____

Bin I.D. Tickets. _____

Analyze Item Activity Report. _____

Cover and order SMS items. _____

Reorder of seasonal items. _____

Order of regular and Deal E factory orders. _____

SECOND WEEK—OPERATIONS

First Day—Office Procedure Learn the system and procedures*, with actual participation of daily cash and sales report.   _____

Register procedure—Actual read-out of registers; use of forms, over and short, employee purchases, state and local taxes, lay-away payment follow-through, handling of cash procedure for any vending machines, rental Blue Lustre machines, other concessions, etc.   _____

Correct handling of sale coupons.   _____

Review of open order file.   _____

Actual working invoices and claims.   _____

Second Day Learn and work the following systems and procedures:

Open to Buy (sample form attached)   _____

Cash Flow (maximum $1,000 on hand—to be covered by insurance)   _____

Markups   _____

Markdowns   _____

Payroll   _____

Set Up of Cash Fund   _____

Personnel Scheduling (worksheet attached)   _____ All Areas

Checkbook Handling   _____ Completed

Bank Reconciliation Form   _____

Payment of Expense Items   _____ _____

Review employee benefits and policies such as sick pay, vacation, insurance, review increases, etc. (Guideline supplement attached).

Third Day Step-by-step review of:

P & L Statement   _____

Merchandise Register   _____

Operating Budget   _____

(Frank discussion of early danger signals and corrective measures to take.) (Should be reviewed 90 days after opening for possible revision by owner and Retail Sales Manager.)

*(Supplement cash office forms attached.)

120   BRANCHING

Expense Register	_____	Completed

Supplemental work sheet on effects of promotions to staples, example attached, plus work sheet to actually work out. _____ _____

Review of all operating forms and function of each. _____

Inventory—Correct procedure for taking inventory (supplement guidelines attached). Inventory control and protection of inventory. _____

Fourth Day Participate in the actual handling of the daily cash routine:

Charge Cards _____

Payment of the Statement terms _____

Special dating of merchandise _____

Relationship between the Statement and the Freight Receiving Book _____

Actual checking off of the Statement _____

Fifth Day The following should be reviewed again:

Daily Cash Routine _____

Seasonal Code Information on Invoices _____

Ben Franklin mailing check-off _____ _____

A review of the first two weeks with "free" time for areas that need further discussion. _____

Sixth Day Home

THIRD WEEK—SALES PROMOTION AND PROFIT

First Day

At this time the Retail Sales Manager should be in the store and actually work and review the new owner's advertising budget, and advertising and promotional plans, with him. As much information as possible should be available to the Trainee/Owner on the town in which he is locating; advertising costs, newspaper distribution, circular cost distribution, etc.

Learn and set up advertising budget _____

How to set up a six-week advertising plan, item selection from monthly Sale Plan, monthly promotional offerings, basic and seasonal Check Lists, etc. _____

Setting up promotional and advertising file, correct handling
of slicks, mats and Sale Plan advertising materials   _____

Poster Service   _____

Second Day Learn end counter profit and productivity control, one-item ends, high-gross ends, seasonal impact ends,
low gross week-end promotions (always maintaining basic-
staple assortment once customer is in the store to offset low
gross promotions), permanent basic-staple ends (Ex.: G.E.   All Areas
Light Bulbs), participate in making advance end plans and   Completed
working on floor with department sales girls. Use floor plan
form attached.   _____

Set up a twelve-month merchandise promotional file.   _____

Third Day

Use Employee Training Film. If employees of trainee store
have not seen this film, arrange their schedules before hand
so they can do so at this time. (Training Film will be made
available to the store by the Retail Sales Manager.)   _____

Conduct weekly employee meeting   _____

Merchandise Turnover and how to figure   _____

Seasonal record-keeping   _____

Advance seasonal buying   _____

Quarterly Return Sheet buying   _____   _____

Fourth Day Complete and thorough discussion of gross
profit, shrinkage control and Ben Franklin's role as a partner
to make the store prosperous.   _____

Review Special Services:

*Advertising	Ad Mat	_____
	Poster Service	_____
*Merchandise	Garden Seeds	_____
	Greeting Card Racks	_____
	Notion Racks	_____
	General Order Program	_____
*General Services	Retail Accounting†	_____
	Electronic Ordering System	_____
	I.D. Tickets	_____ All Areas
	Pre-Printed Price Labels	_____ Completed
	Item Activity Report	_____

*(Supplement Forms and Information Sheets attached.)
†(Full review with Retail Accounting Manager, 4th week, 4th day.)

How to handle authorized Reps calling on stores.   ———

Proper handling will-follow items and cancellations; handling of weekly price changes.   ———

Chicago Pool shipments and ordering procedure; Timex watches, Matchbox cars.   ———

Over-the-counter warranty; return procedures.   ———

Handling of late factory orders; proper follow-up procedure.
                                                                    ———

Fifth Day A visit from the Retail Sales Manager to cover all of his functions and responsibilities and how it all relates between stores, region and headquarters*; a review of what the owner has covered in the first three weeks and answering any questions he may have; purpose and use of Regional/National Advisory Board.   ———

Six Day Check and place store's weekly orders:

E.O.S. Check List   ———

Seasonal   ———

Sale Plan   ———

Actually handle transmission of orders, adjusting this schedule to transmitting day, if necessary.   ———

Visual checking of key factory sources for replacement orders.   ———

Saturday week-end traffic check; observe personal service, checkout performance, handle cash pickups, bank deposit.
                                                                    ———

FOURTH WEEK

First Day A one-half day visit from Apparel Coordinator and a one-half day visit from Fabric/Homecraft Coordinator; review of Coordinator's specific areas, merchandise offerings, record keeping, return sheets, factory follow-up procedure.   ———

Importance of attending Spring/Fall Merchandise Shows.   ———

Apparel Coordinator (Outline of things to be covered given below.   ———

Fabric/Homecraft Coordinator (Outline of things to be covered given below).   ———

*Regional-Headquarters organization flow charts attached.

(including the Occupation-Safety-Health Act requirements —copy of OSHA from the state of new owner's location will be made available); actually participate in handling of daily cash, checking or making entries; briefly review Weeks 1, 2 and 3, especially areas that need further explanation.

Third Day Review the pre-opening of a new store. (If a Ben Franklin store is opening in the immediate area during this four-week orientation period, this schedule should be adjusted so a visit can be made.) At this time review only the store being visited. Do not get into the trainee/owner's pre-opening. This will be handled by the Retail Sales Manager in detail.

_____

This should include Merchandise-Fixture planning, merchandising procedure, manager's role in store opening, employee hiring, scheduling, training, payroll control, advertising, pre-planning after opening, promotional and advertising program.

_____

Fourth Day A visit from the Retail Accounting Manager, with a full discussion of Ben Franklin retail accounting procedures.

_____

Fifth Day An open review covering the four-week indoctrination.

_____

FIFTH WEEK

New owner will be scheduled to re-visit the regional distribution center prior to going into his store.

_____

NEW STORE OWNER APPAREL TRAINING PROGRAM

Place a check in the right-hand column when the scheduled item is completed and understood.

1. Introduction and explanation of the Regional Apparel
   Coordinator's function:
   Apparel Coordinator's Name: _____
   Address: _____
   _____
   Phone:_____   _____

2. Explanation of merchandise philosophy and buying techniques of
   the Headquarters Apparel Buying Division.   _____

3. Explanation of the Headquarters Store Operations Division and the
   responsibilities of the Headquarters Apparel Coordinator.   _____

4. Completely review the Apparel Manual. Trainee should be encouraged to use this manual in training new employees.   _____

5. These areas should be covered with the trainee. Check (✓) where
   provided when you feel the subject has been completely covered
   and understood.

   a. Departments
      Explanation
      List of Apparel Departments   _____

   b. Merchandise Presentation
      In-Store Presentation
      Sizing Colorizing   _____

   c. Return Sheet
      Benefits
      Schedule
      Instructions
      Return Sheet Claims   _____

   d. Seasonal Listings
      Purpose
      Instructions   _____

   e. Fashion Mailing
      Purpose
      Instructions   _____

   f. Fashion News
      Fashion Tip
      Items on the Move

Buyers Notes   _____

g. Basic Check Lists
       Purpose
       Instructions   _____

h. Record Keeping
       Basic Records
       Item Performance Record Sheets   _____

i. Markdowns
       How to Avoid
       Seasonal Clearance
       12-Month Program   _____

j. Claims
       Defective Merchandise
       Other Returns   _____

k. Advertising
       Apparel Advertising Service
       Sale Plans   _____

Points *a* through *k* are individual chapters to be found within the Apparel Manual. Be sure to refer to the manual when reviewing these subjects.

NEW STORE OWNER FABRIC TRAINING PROGRAM

Place a check in the right-hand column when the scheduled item is completed and understood.

1. Introduction and explanation of the Regional Fabric
   Coordinator's function:
   Fabric Coordinator's Name:_____
   Address: _____
   _____
   Phone:_____ _____

2. Spring and Fall Seasonal Package—Explain how we obtain our merchandise and review the various firms we deal with. _____

3. A & P Sublines—How it is set up and how it operates. _____

4. Types of fixtures and setting fixtures—Pages 2 to 7* _____

5. Marking Merchandise—Page 7 _____

6. Displays—Show how to fold and drape fabrics—Page 8 _____

7. Mannequins—Proper use and value to department—Page 9 _____

8. Signs and Image of department—Page 11 _____

9. Shortage and defective merchandise—Pages 16 and 18 _____

10. Inventories—Page 17 _____

11. Markdowns—Page 21 _____

12. Remnant Program and value to department—Page 22 _____

13. Advertising and promotions—Pages 23 and 24 _____

14. Record keeping—Page 27 _____

*Reference page numbers refer to pages in the Fabric Manual.

HYPOTHETICAL BRANCH OPERATOR RECRUITMENT PROJECTIONS

Program "Arithmetic"

The following pages contain examples of arithmetical projections. These show estimated cost and income factors for both the parent and the associate.

It should be stressed that during the preliminary conceptual stages (prior to a track record having been achieved), these projections are necessarily "assumptive." They are designed to provide preliminary guidelines or estimates of (1) what the program will cost during the various stages of program implementation and (2) what income can be expected pursuant to actual operating experience.

In establishing costs we take into consideration:

Estimated recruitment pace (acquisition of associates)

Costs for establishing each associate

Projected expenses

Table 8-1 contains projections over a 4-year period. You'll note from this table that the recruitment pace accelerates each year as experience and track record increase.

TABLE 8-1 Projected Quarterly Operator Sales over 4-Year Period

		Sales		
Year	Quarter	Quarterly accumulation	Annual accumulation	Total
1	1	—	—	—
	2	3	3	3
	3	6	9	9
	4	9	18	18
2	1	5	5	23
	2	6	11	29
	3	7	18	36
	4	9	27	45
3	1	7	7	52
	2	8	15	60
	3	9	24	69
	4	11	35	80
4	1	7	7	87
	2	8	15	95
	3	9	24	104
	4	11	35	115

TABLE 8-2 Estimated Turnkey Building and Equipment Cost, 200-Seat Facility

Cost factors	Dollars
Land	135,000
Building	185,000
Lot work	30,000
Equipment	75,000
Total cost	425,000

TABLE 8-3 Estimated Capital Required for Industry Entry by Branch Operator, 200-Seat Capacity

	Capital required	
	Total investment	Cash required
Branchise fee	$15,000	$ 15,000
Equipment package*	75,000	25,000
Supplies (basic inventory)	10,000	10,000
Security on leasehold	5,000	5,000
Working capital	10,000	10,000
Total	$115,000	$65,000

*Balance of $55,000 on equipment to be financed over a 5-year period.

TABLE 8-4 Projected Operator's Profit and Loss at the Gross Sales Level of $500,000

	Dollars	Percent of total sales
Gross sales	500,000	100.0
Cost of goods sold:		
Food	219,000	43.8
Paper	10,000	2.0
Total cost of goods sold	229,000	45.8
Gross margin	271,000	54.2
Total expenses	225,000	45.0
Net profit B/T	46,000	9.2
Expenses		
Payroll and taxes	100,000	20.0
Laundry and supplies	7,000	1.4
Utilities and telephone	15,000	3.0
Property taxes	3,000	.6
Insurance	2,000	.4
Maintenance and repairs	4,000	.8
Advertising	15,000	3.0
Office expenses	1,000	.2
Royalties	20,000	4.0
Rent	40,000	8.0
Breakage	3,000	.6
Miscellaneous	2,000	.4
Professional fees	1,000	.2
Interest expense*	4,500	.9
Equipment depreciation†	7,500	1.5
Total expenses	225,000	45.0

*Interest rate on the $50,000 equipment package financing reflects a 8.5% to 9.0% add-on to going rate.
†Equipment depreciation is calculated on a basis of straight-line depreciation over a 10-year period.

TABLE 8-5 Projected Operator's Profit and Loss at the Gross Sales Level of $600,000

	Dollars	Percent of total sales
Gross sales	600,000	100.0
Cost of goods sold:		
Food	262,800	43.8
Paper	12,000	2.0
Total cost of goods sold	274,800	45.8
Gross margin	325,200	54.2
Total expenses	259,200	43.2
Net profit B/T	66,000	11.0
Expenses		
Payroll and taxes	114,000	19.0
Laundry and supplies	7,800	1.3
Utilities and telephone	16,800	2.8
Property taxes	3,600	.6
Insurance	2,400	.4
Maintenance and repairs	4,200	.7
Advertising	18,000	3.0
Office expenses	1,200	.2
Royalties	24,000	4.0
Rent	48,000	8.0
Breakage	3,600	.6
Miscellaneous	2,400	.4
Professional fees	1,200	.2
Interest expenses	4,500	.75
Equipment depreciation	7,500	1.25
Total expenses	259,200	43.20

TABLE 8-6 Projected Cost of Placing One Branch Owner/Operator into the Business

Cost to operator		
Branchisee fee		$15,000
Cost to parent*		
Site selection	$2,500	
Recruitment advertising	1,000	
Branchise salesperson	3,000	
Schooling and training	5,000	
Legal	1,000	
Total cost to parent	$12,500	12,500
Balance retained by parent company		$ 2,500

*These costs will drop by economies of scale.

TABLE 8-8 Projected Quarterly Gross Income*, in Dollars, to Parent Company from Royalties (4%), 4-Year Period

Year	Quarters				Total
	1	2	3	4	
1	. . . . .	. . . . .	. . . . .	9,600	9,600
2	33,600	72,000	100,800	129,600	336,000
3	160,000	201,600	236,800	273,600	872,000
4	316,800	364,800	404,800	441,600	1,528,000

*Figures are calculated on $1600 per month per store.

TABLE 8-7 Projected Quarterly Gross Income to Parent Company from Sale of Branch Interests, 4-Year Period

Year	Quarters				Total
	1	2	3	4	
1	. . . . .	45,000	90,000	135,000	270,000
2	75,000	90,000	105,000	135,000	405,000
3	105,000	120,000	135,000	165,000	525,000
4	105,000	120,000	135,000	165,000	525,000

TABLE 8-9 Projected Quarterly Gross Income*, in Dollars, to Parent Company from Equipment Markup† and Plant Construction‡, 4-Year Period

Year	Quarters 1	2	3	4	Total
1	. . . . .	. . . . .	. . . . .	45,000	45,000
2	90,000	135,000	75,000	90,000	390,000
3	105,000	135,000	105,000	120,000	465,000
4	135,000	165,000	105,000	120,000	525,000

*Figures are calculated on $15,000 per store.
†Equipment markup is 10% or $7,500 per unit.
‡Profit from plant construction is 4% or $7,450 per unit.

TABLE 8-10 Projected Quarterly Gross Income*, in Dollars, to Parent Company from Leasing Operation†, 4-Year Period

Year	Quarters 1	2	3	4	Total
1	. . . . .	. . . . .	. . . . .	19,800	19,800
2	69,300	148,500	207,900	267,300	693,000
3	330,000	415,800	488,400	564,300	1,798,500
4	653,400	752,400	834,900	910,800	3,151,500

*Figures are calculated on $3300 per month per store.
†The rentals were calculated on the basis of parent company receiving a minimum of 10% on land and 13% on building as its return on investment. This is reflected in the $40,000 rental (Table 8-4) which parent receives from operator against 8% of gross sales.

TABLE 8-11 Projected Quarterly Gross Income*, in Dollars, to Parent Company from Miscellaneous Income Sources (1%),† 4-Year Period

Year	Quarters 1	2	3	4	Total
1	. . . . .	18,000	. . . . .	2,400	20,400
2	8,400	18,000	25,200	32,400	84,000
3	40,000	50,400	59,200	68,400	218,000
4	79,200	91,200	101,200	110,400	382,000

*Figures are calculated on $400 per month per store.
†Miscellaneous refers to parent company income from the operator for performing services and supplying needs of operator. Such needs and services are beyond the requirements, justifying the royalty fee.

THE QUALIFICATION FORM FOR PROSPECTIVE BRANCH OPERATORS

The "qualification form" is a useful tool for the parent company. It serves a number of purposes, the principal ones being as follows:

To Discourage Nonserious Applications. The applicant who is mainly interested in accumulating a lot of literature will normally not fill out detailed forms. These "professional" applicants like to get a lot of mail, perhaps to impress others or just to give themselves a feeling of importance. At any rate they waste your time and money. Any serious applicant does not mind filling out the necessary information.

To Screen out Unqualified Applicants. It provides a "quick look at the person" that can save time and money by eliminating unnecessary interviews and lengthy correspondence. If the individual is obviously unqualified, you can eliminate him with a polite form letter saying "thank you."

As a Basis for Conducting the Interview. When an applicant looks like a good prospect whom you wish to interview, the qualification form gives the interviewer something concrete to discuss with the prospect and serves as a basis for further inquiry.

As a Source of Credit Information. This provides important data when an extension of credit and financing is built into your program.

Titles of the Qualification Form

Analysis of some eighty different forms used by leading franchisors shows a variety of titles. Among them are:

Confidential information form
Personal history
Confidential application
Application
Preinterview form
Qualification report

Confidential "get-acquainted" application form
Credit application
Application for interview form
Request for interview

They are all different ways of describing the same thing. No special title is recommended. It is a matter of the personal taste of the company.

Size of the Qualification Form

The typical qualification form in use is a single sheet, 8½-by-11, printed on one side, with the other side usable for additional information. However, a number of forms are printed on both sides. A few companies use very detailed forms including four or more pages, but these are rare.

Checklist of Information to Be Asked for, by Category

The following items represent a composite of what the majority of companies, whose forms were used in this survey, asked for. This should prove a useful checklist about the design of a form as well as for those who might be thinking of revising the old form.

PERSONAL INFORMATION

Name _____

Address _____

City _____Zone _____State _____Zip Code _____

Telephone _____Area Code _____

How long have you lived in this city? _____

How long at the present address? _____

Previous Address How Long? _____

Age _____Birthplace _____

Are you a U.S. Citizen? _____

Marital Status_____

Spouse's name _____

Number of dependent children _____Ages_____

Do you have any physical defects? _____Explain _____

_____

List any serious illnesses during the past 10 years _____

_____

Education: High School Graduate( ) College, 1 2 3 4 yrs. Degree _____

Do you own your own home?_____Is it mortgaged? _____

Names of banks: Personal checking _____

Personal savings _____

Business account _____

Have you ever been bonded?_____For how much? $ _____

Have you ever been refused bond?_____Explain _____

Have you ever gone bankrupt?_____For how much $ _____

_____Explain date and circumstances _____

_____

Do you have any outstanding liabilities resulting from previous failures?_____

_____Explain _____

Amount of Life Insurance carried $ _____

Do you own a car?_____Make and model_____

Capital available to invest $ _____

Current income level ( ) $10,000 or less ( ) $10,000–$15,000

( ) $15,000–$20,000 ( ) $20,000 or more

Are you able to carry yourself for at least 6 months?_____

ASSETS

Cash . . . . $_____

Securities . . . . $_____

Real Estate. . . . . $_____

Auto . . . . $_____

Other (describe). . . . . $_____

TOTAL ASSETS . . . . . $_____

LIABILITIES

Accounts Payable . . . . . $_____

Notes Payable. . . . . . . $_____

Installment accts. . . . . . $_____

Other (describe). . . . . . $_____

_____

TOTAL LIABILITIES . . . . . $_____

Are you an endorser on notes, mortgages, bonds or other obligations for others? _____Explain _____

EXPERIENCE INFORMATION

Business Experience or Jobs Last 5 Years (Latest First)

Period	Company & Address	Type of Business	Duties

Note: No previous employers will be contacted without your permission.

Describe your most valuable (in your opinion) executive experience _____

_____

Elaborate on important sales or sales manager experience_____

_____

Military experience _____

_____

YOU AND US

Territory preference _____

Second choice _____

Would your business be owned and actively operated by yourself? _____

By you and a partner?_____By you and your wife? _____

Explain, if not owned and operated by yourself _____

Would you have any other business interests?_____Explain in detail _____

_____

If approved, how soon can you start? _____

ACTIVITIES INFORMATION

List organizations, clubs, fraternal and social activities that you are affiliated with and how active a part you take.

_____

_____

_____

REFERENCE INFORMATION

Personal references (not former employers or relatives)

1 _____

2 _____

Credit references (other than bank)

1 _____

2 _____

Note: References will not be contacted without your permission.

I understand that the above information will be held in the strictest confidence, and that this form incurs no obligation on either party. *Additional information contained on separate sheet*

Date_____Signature_____

Field Representative _____

Do Not Write in this Space

Field Representative's remarks _____

( ) Accepted   ( ) Rejected because _____

PRELIMINARY "GET-ACQUAINTED" FACT SHEET

CONFIDENTIAL

Note: Completing this form does not obligate you or us in any way. It merely is intended to provide information on which to base preliminary discussions. All information will be kept strictly confidential and no verification of references or statements will be made until negotiations progress.

Fill in and mail to
President

Figure 8-1 Get Aquainted fact sheet

THIS IS NOT A CONTRACT

PERSONAL DATA

Date_____

Name_____

HOME PHONE	
area code	number

Residence Address_____

City_____State_____Zip_____

Age_____Health_____Physical Impairments_____

Married ☐ Single ☐ Divorce ☐ Widowed ☐ Dependents_____

Names of Fraternal, business, civic organizations to which you belong_____

_____

_____

BUSINESS DATA

Your present business or corporation_____

Your position_____Telephone_____

Type of business_____

Business Address_____

City_____State_____Zip_____

How long in this business_____Annual Salary_____

Previous Business history_____

_____

_____

_____

Have you ever been bonded? Yes ☐   No☐   Amount $_____

REFERENCES

Business Bank_____

Branch_____Address_____

Savings Bank_____

Branch_____Address_____

Name_____Relationship_____

Address_____

Name_____ Relationship_____

Address_____

Figure 8-1

CONFIDENTIAL DATA

FINANCIAL DATA

Your average annual income for the past 5 years?_____per year.

YOUR ASSETS (at current market value)		YOUR LIABILITIES	
Cash on hand	$_____	Notes payable to banks	$_____
Cash in banks	$_____	Other notes payable	$_____
Notes receivable	$_____	Accounts payable	$_____
Loans receivable	$_____	Loans against Life Insurance	$_____
Life Insurance — cash value	$_____	Real estate mortgages payable	$_____
Securities — listed marketable	$_____	Taxes payable	$_____
Mortgages owned	$_____	Interest payable	$_____
Real estate	$_____	Brokers margin accounts	$_____
Automobiles	$_____	Other liabilities	$_____
Other assets	$_____	....	$_____
....	$_____	....	$_____
....	$_____	....	$_____
TOTAL ASSETS	$_____	Total Liabilities	$_____
		NET WORTH	$_____

CONTEMPLATED ENTERPRISE

Do you have a preference as to area or city where you would like to locate your franchise?
Yes ( )   No ( )
List areas in order of preference:

1._____   3._____

2._____   4._____

Investment structure: Individual ☐ Partnership ☐ Syndicate ☐ Investment Group ☐

Other principles, in addition to yourself:

Name_____% of interest_____

Address_____Telephone_____

City_____State_____Zip_____

Name_____% of interest_____

Address_____Telephone_____

City_____State_____Zip_____

(if additional space is needed, use back page and check here ☐)

NOTE: Completing this form does not obligate you or us in any way. It is intended only to provide information on which to base preliminary discussions. All information will be kept strictly confidential and no verification of statements or references will be made until negotiations are initiated.

THIS IS NOT A CONTRACT   Signature_____

Figure 8-1

GETTING TO KNOW YOU INTERNATIONAL, LTD.
525 NORTHERN BOULEVARD, GREAT NECK, NEW YORK 11021

Confidential "Get-Acquainted" Application Form

PERSONAL

Name..
Please Print

Address...

City...State...........

Telephone...

How long have you lived in city?.........................How long at present address? ....

Previous address ....How long?...................

Age.............Marital Status.......................

Wife's Name..

Number of dependent Children...............

FINANCIAL

Do you own your home?......................

Name of bank..

Have you ever been bonded?...For how much? $................

Have you ever been refused a bond?.................Reason..........................

Have you ever gone bankrupt?.............When?.......................For how much? $................

Checking ☐
Savings ☐
Both ☐

YOU AND IRAD

Territory preference ....

What other territory would you consider?......................................

Do you realize that this is a full-time business? ....

Is there any doubt in your mind that you are capable of handling a distributorship of this kind?.........

If so, what?......................................

If approved, how soon can you enter our training program?......................

ACTIVITIES

List all organizations, clubs, fraternal and social activities that you are affiliated with, and how active a part you take. Comment briefly on your present and previous business experience.

REFERENCE

Names and Addresses of 2 Character References (not related to you):

1. ....

2. ....

NOTE: References will not be contacted without your permission.

DO NOT WRITE IN THIS SPACE

Rejected ( ) ....

Accepted ( ) If Rejected, give reasons ....

I understand that this is NOT a contract, and this form incurs no obligation on either party.
I certify that the above information is complete and correct.

Applicant's Signature..

Field Representative..............................   Date..............................

Figure 8-2

BELL TELEVISION SURVEY
EDUCATIONAL-TV INFORMATION SHEET

☐ **EXISTING building**

☐ **NEW construction**

E

Number of CAMERAS	Model Number	RF Channel	VIDEO	LENSES

☐ **CONSOLE**   ☐ **NO CONSOLE**

REMARKS:

☐ **See Other Side**

Number of MONITORS	Types, Screen Size	RF Channel	VIDEO	LOCATIONS

Number of TRIPODS	Type

Number of DOLLIES	Type

✔

- Sound Modulator for RF camera
- "A" Scope
- Tally Lights
- Switching: ☐ Relays   ☐ Selector
- Audio Video Mixer
- Class Room TV Stands
- Class Room Ceiling Mounts

ESTIMATED COSTS

	DISTRIBUTOR'S COST	SUGGESTED SELLING PRICE
MATERIAL	$	$
MAN HOURS HRS.	$	$
GUARANTEE MOS.	$	$
DISTRIBUTOR'S TOTAL COST	$	
SUGGESTED QUOTATION		$

Copies: ☐ HOME OFFICE   ☐ DISTRIB.   ☐ SALESMAN

Figure 8-3

FACT-GATHERING FORMS

It is the objective of the parent company to assist associates to make maximum sales and earnings. To accomplish this, the successful parent will endeavor to fulfill those functions that may distract the associate, e.g., estimating, installing, etc. Ordinarily these factors do not conform to the skills of a sales-oriented associate. To compile the intricate figures and other criteria needed to prepare an adequate estimate might take days and could seriously curtail the associate's sales time and potential.

To expedite the fulfillment of these operations, the parent company should prepare and provide self-check forms enabling the associate to "check off" important work specifications while on the spot. This can normally be done in a matter of minutes. The parent has the expertise to evaluate this checked off data and subsequently to prepare a prompt and accurate estimate in behalf of the customer. Hence the parent performs in behalf of the associate an important function that acts to cement their relationship; the associate is resultantly "unleashed" to spend most of his time in sales and earnings.

Installation should also be prearranged with outside factors who will agree to do work for a fixed, designated fee. For example, in the instance of sauna baths, carpenters and electricians were appointed on a local basis for a prearranged installation fee. In the case of closed-circuit television, local electricians were appointed.

Figures 8-4 and 8-5 are examples of fact-gathering forms provided to Branchisees to expedite preparation of proposals. These also enable Branchisors to assist Branchisees in accurate proposal preparation.

BELL TELEVISION SURVEY
MASTER ANTENNA INFORMATION SHEET

☐ **EXISTING building**

☐ **NEW construction**

A

Distributor's Sequence #

FOR HOME OFFICE USE

Home Office Sequence #

Number of IDENTICAL buildings	Number STORIES with apartments
Maximum number OUTLETS per apt.	Maximum number OUTLETS PER FLOOR
TOTAL NUMBER OUTLETS PER BUILDING	

Number CONDUITS for MAS	Number conduits BACK-TO-BACK
Number COAX. RISERS	Number SINGLE cond. not back-to-back

ANTENNAS:
Check or list all channels to be received

VHF Channel #	FREQUENCY (Megacycles)	CALL LETTERS	Airline Miles from Building
2	54-60		
3	60-66		
4	66-72		
5	76-82		
6	82-88		
7	174-180		
8	180-186		
9	186-192		
10	192-198		
11	198-204		
12	204-210		
13	210-216		
FM	88-108	All Stations	
AM	.5-1.6	All Stations	
UHF-			
UHF-			
UHF-			
UHF-			

REMARKS: ☐ **See Other Side**

ESTIMATED COSTS

	DISTRIBUTOR'S COST	SUGGESTED SELLING PRICE
MATERIAL	$	$
MAN HOURS HRS.	$	$
GUARANTEE MOS.	$	$
DISTRIBUTOR'S TOTAL COST	$	
SUGGESTED QUOTATION		$

Copies: | HOME OFFICE | | DISTRIB. | | SALESMAN |

Figure 8-4

BELL TELEVISION SURVEY
EDUCATIONAL-TV INFORMATION SHEET

☐ EXISTING building

☐ NEW construction

E

Distributor's Sequence #

FOR HOME OFFICE USE

Home Office Sequence #

Number of CAMERAS	Model Number	RF Channel	VIDEO	LENSES

☐ CONSOLE   ☐ NO CONSOLE

Number of MONITORS	Types, Screen Size	RF Channel	VIDEO	LOCATIONS

REMARKS:

☐ See Other Side

Number of TRIPODS	Type	Number of DOLLIES	Type

✔	
Sound Modulator for RF camera	
"A" Scope	
Tally Lights	
Switching: ☐ Relays ☐ Selector	
Audio Video Mixer	
Class Room TV Stands	
Class Room Ceiling Mounts	

ESTIMATED COSTS

	DISTRIBUTOR'S COST	SUGGESTED SELLING PRICE
MATERIAL	$	$
MAN HOURS HRS.	$	$
GUARANTEE MOS.	$	$
DISTRIBUTOR'S TOTAL COST	$	
SUGGESTED QUOTATION		$

Copies: | HOME OFFICE | | DISTRIB. | | SALESMAN |

Figure 8-5

Promotions

From the moment the Branchisee signs his contract, your work as the Branchisor really commences. It is your job to make him successful. If you do, then Branchising will repay you well—the profits can be almost unlimited. If you do not, then Branchising can be grim, unprofitable, and (as many American Branchisors have discovered) litigation plagued.

The success of any Branchise program is:

NOT the number of colored tacks that you may have attached to your office sales map

NOT the great numbers of Branchisees you have obtained that you proudly point to

NOT even the size of your initial Branchisee fee

No, it is none of these. Whether you have only 2 Branchisees or 250, the success of your program is based only on how successful they are.

Never look at the initial Branchisee fee that you charge as your source for profit. This fee—no matter how big it is—quickly fritters away in trying to remake a wrong program into a right one. The big earnings you seek can only come from the *successful* Branchisees you have.

Therefore, a discussion of the types of concepts—the type of innovativeness—needed to help Branchisees compete in the present-day market and to succeed is critical. The plans offered are also applicable to nonbranchised businesses; these plans represent the newest methods attuned to today's marketplace and have achieved substantial earnings for other companies over the world. And, most importantly, they are methods that, in almost each instance, do not require increased overhead.

BRANCH OFFICES

As many as one hundred branch offices can be acquired by your Branchisees. There are several excellent methods for achieving this:

Catalog Corners. Only your own store will display merchandise. This means that tables to which the Branchisee's catalog is attached are placed in other (noncompet-

ing) stores throughout the area, with the participating storekeeper obtaining a commission on referrals coming from his store. Your catalogs are also placed in train and plane depots where large crowds congregate. Thus the Branchisee now has *marketwide* exposure, on a prestigious level, giving him in effect dozens of branch offices without increasing his own overhead.

Such well-known stores like Sears, Roebuck & Co., J. C. Penney, and even Macy's have featured such catalog corners with extremely profitable results.

Stand-up Signs. Companies that have no catalogs—such as service-type operations—place an attractive stand-up sign in noncompetitive stores throughout the area, each participating dealer receiving a commission on referrals. This plan was used for a client who had a service-type operation that offered a gardening service to homes. The results greatly increased his sales, besides providing valuable advertising and public relations exposure.

Product Displays. Place *displays* of your products or services in noncompeting stores in your area. For example, a cosmetics manufacturer placed cosmetic displays in drugstores; a candy maker placed candy displays in drugstores; a wig maker contacted all the barber and the beauty salons in his area and literally achieved hundreds of branch offices; and a boutique wholesaler contacted all the hotels in his area and installed his boutique displays in their lobbies. A local pipe shop had displays of its expensive pipes in a hotel we recently stayed in and had displays in other hotels as well. An art gallery also displayed samples of its paintings in several hotels. The same idea is applicable to many types of products— and to services, too.

Tie-in Businesses. Whenever you can, try to tie in your business with another one. A Branchise that used high-pressure spraying equipment to clean roofs, chimneys, gutters, driveways, and homes participated with a chain of national department stores to promote these services with its customer list.

Ads in Telephone Books. Another method of obtaining *branch offices* is to place your advertisements in telephone books throughout your trading area—not in just the particular city where you are located—thus reaching inaccessible areas that need, but do not know where to obtain, your products or services.

If you think that this "branch office" concept is too novel or too unorthodox, consider this fact: In the United States, one of the most prestigious stores in the men's apparel field is Brooks Brothers. Many of you may have heard of them. Their patronage is so highly selective that it has been humorously stated one needs to show proof of a bank account of at least $100,000 and to have impeccable character references before they'll even allow you to buy from them! Yet, recently, this same firm—with all its dignity—has been renting hotel rooms throughout the country to display and sell their merchandise (similar to the way suits from Hong Kong have been sold). Again, they have given themselves the benefit of many branch offices.

SALESPEOPLE

Get all the clubs, churches, and other associations in a community to promote actively the sale of your products or services. The reason such organizations will cooperate is because each has an *earnings funds* program to earn monies to finance charities and other worthwhile projects. That means that hundreds of their members will actively sell your products for you to their friends, neighbors, and others.

A client in the light-bulb field obtained such earnings funds participation from the Junior Chambers of Commerce and the Kiwanis, Lions, Rotary, and Elks clubs; this gave him over a thousand salespeople! As a result sales totaled $400,000 just from these sources.

Even girl scouts and boy scouts are helpful. They will knock on doors throughout the area and project their wonderful, heart-warming personalities, just selling for you.

NEW, SEPARATE BUSINESSES

You can add three, six, and even more new, separate businesses to your present basic business without changing your business concept or image.

Consider your basic business: What "new departments" can profitably be added to it?

Mail-Order Department.   This enables you to reach customers who would not ordinarily come to your store. It enables you to achieve a "new dimension" in your business and to obtain complete market coverage. For example, a Branchisor in the bookstore field added a mail-order department; the mail-order section of his business did better than his store sales and, in fact, helped to increase his retail sales. A Branchisor in the jewelry field also built up a thriving mail-order business, offering gift and jewelry items. What can be mail ordered in *your* business?

Rent It Department.   In addition to selling your products, consider *renting* them. Here is a simple idea that has helped many small businesses to multiply their sales. The success of this plan is based on a simple point of psychology: Many people hesitate to commit themselves on a "big" purchase, but they're willing to spend less money to "try it out." Generally, they end up by buying it. For example, appliance stores rent TV sets for so much per day with these payments credited to the purchase price; office machine stores rent typewriters, bookkeeping machines, dictaphone machines, etc.; and music shops rent pianos. This idea has been used by practically any type of business: auto dealers, hardware stores, sporting goods stores, etc.

Added Related Products or Services.   Evaluate the nature of your product or service. What related product or service can be added so that your Branchisee can increase his earnings by selling to the same customer? For example, a tobacco store added boutiques and greeting cards. In the service field, a Branchised business that cleaned roofs, driveways, chimneys, and patios with water and chemical sprays added other home-related businesses: spray fire deterrents and spray paints—and even customized concrete steps (since this also pertained to homes).

Think about your own products or services: What related products or departments can be attached to them to enhance the earning potential of your Branchisees?

Still another approach for reaching out of your store (or other place of business) to help cover your total market is to add "mobility" to your business. Equip a motor van to sell and service the customers right at their own homes. For example, there was the "pet mobile" of a Branchise pet shop that was fully equipped to groom poodles and other dogs right in the van; it made regular rounds of their customers' homes. There was also a fully equipped "handyman mobile" of a hardware dealer that contacted homes in each area to perform their needed services.

Another example is the spray painting of homes offered by a Branchised paint dealer; a motor van was especially equipped to perform this work. Many of you have heard of Snap-on Tools. The business of this highly successful Branchised organization is essentially built around a truck bringing tools and accessories to garages, gas stations, and auto dealers on a regular schedule.

GREATER INVENTORY

Provide the advantage of greater inventory without having to actually increase your inventory. This concept, on its face value, sounds so preposterous that perhaps it is best explained by the example of a Branchisor in the bookstore field. Normally, as much as $60,000 in inventory is required to equip such a store, which would be altogether too costly for the planned mom-and-pop Branchise. Instead, the Branchisor improved his distribution methods by computerizing them, so that stock replacement shipments were made the same day instead of 30 days later. Thus the dealer with the same assortment of books could now order one-fifth his usual requirements. This meant that he could open a store with as little as $10,000 in inventory. It furthermore meant that instead of only two turnovers a year he could have as many as ten. He also arranged a special department in each dealer's store displaying the Branchisor's catalog and inviting catalog orders. The catalog contained $250,000 in inventory, giving each dealer the benefit of showing that amount in merchandise to customers. Hence this same, small $10,000-inventory store, in effect, became a $250,000-inventory store, surpassing the stock of any competitor in its field.

As you may know, such chain store giants, such as Sears, Roebuck and Montgomery Ward, also have catalog-ordering departments.

ATTRACTING THE CUSTOMERS

Get your best customers to come to you in large groups.

Arrange Convention Exhibits. I am referring to business conventions, associations, trade unions, and so on. There is the example of the Branchisor who provides record-keeping systems for the medical profession: Rather than selling one system at a time from physician to physician, he contacted groups of physicians at conventions and was able to talk and sell to as many as a hundred or more prospects at one time. Supplementing this, he set up exhibits at professional conventions.

There is another example of a client in the motivational field who contacted labor unions, a source that most organizations ignore. Today, unions have large funds available to help "uplift" their members. In contacting only three such unions, which is only a fraction of the total union membership, he was able to sell motivational programs for use by some 6000 union members.

Conducting Seminars.   One example is a Branchisor in the field of communications who manufactured and sold office telephones that replaced the public telephone system. This equipment enabled firms, such as department stores and other large organizations, to save substantial monies in addition to obtaining a better service. A seminar was announced to the foremost companies among the *Fortune* magazine "500" (comprising the largest organizations in the states). A substantial number of top executives attended because the subject was appealing: "Achieving Better Communications in Your Organization and Saving as Much as $50,000 a Year." It was, in fact, the kind of subject and the kind of authoritative panel that were so appealing they would have gladly paid a fee to attend!

Conducting Exhibits.   This is another means to bring your products or services before large groups. Exhibits held in trade shows, conventions, state and city fairs, and the like are most useful. Also, local, Branchisee-conducted exhibits, held in either the Branchisee's store, office, or hotel room, are helpful. Prospective customers are invited to attend. It can include such facets as a flower shop that advised women about various kinds of flowers and floral arrangements and how they can be used for home display and table decorations to fit any desired need. Furniture and decorating shops exhibited pictures of the newest furniture designs, discussed varied period designs, the combining of colors, etc. A hardware store conducted a special showing of items that help women save space around the home.

REACHING EVERY PROSPECT

Reach every prospect in your community, in both homes and businesses without adding any salaried employees: Direct-to-customer marketing is a multibillion-dollar business in the United States. Some of the largest department stores and other organizations now recognize the effectiveness of direct-to-customer approaches. These include such renowned stores as Macy's, Gimbels, and others. They offer in-home service for such items as interior decoration, upholstery, draperies, modernization, furniture, apparel, and dozens of other products and services. A recent ad by Gimbels even offered termite protection services on a shop-at-home basis.

TAKE AN OBJECTIVE LOOK AT "YOU"

Walking in the famous "pushcart" section of Manhattan with one ramshackle cart after another showing a great variety of merchandise, we saw one pushcart that stood out in particular. Its merchandise baffled description. It was really a pile of junk—yes, actually so—for example, an old razor, a rusty handle for a drawer, an old key, a broken toy. Who would ever buy the stuff? But the pushcart proprietor didn't look at his merchandise as "junk." He handled each piece as if it was a rare jewel, picking up the rusty razor with spotlessly white tissue paper, almost like a jeweler displaying a $1-million diamond. Somehow the "value image" communicated itself to people around the stand. They started buying the rusty nail, the razor, the old key, and the old picture frame. They didn't buy the product, they bought the "dream"; not what the product was, but what it could be!

Look at your business! If it is a hardware store, it is just "another" store, so to speak, competing with many similar ones. It necessitates the offering of competitive prices or leaning upon neighborhood loyalty for patronage, neither of these alternatives being dependable.

However, utilize this same hardware store. Plan to sell "systems" rather than "products." Change its concept to a "Store for Better Living," *"better living"* that offers:

Better-equipped kitchens	Safety
Increased home conveniences	Home security
Durability	Increased home value

By selling *systems,* you dramatize the effect of your products: The things they can *do* rather than the things they *are.* It allows you to sell your products in *clusters,* a number at a time, instead of one by one. It also enables you to offer a concept that no competitor has. Think about *your* store and about what systems you can offer. For example, a Branchisor in the lighting field, whose products included lamps of all types, offered a complete lighting system for homes and offices. He now sold "better vision" and "better working efficiency" rather than a product. A manufacturer of door locks offered a complete "home security system" which included proper locks and other security precautions for the entire home, including installation.

A Branchisor of record-keeping books offered a complete business management system that had all the books and forms needed to assist the businessperson in both keeping proper records and managing his business.

SUMMARY

All these new concepts give an "added dimension" to the business of your Branchisees. The patronage attracted by the store itself becomes secondary. The substantial business is obtained through the promotions used outside the store to bring your products or services direct to the prospective purchaser in the most dramatic, effective manner.

Finally, and very importantly, look in your role of Branchisor or home office at your own establishment. Are *you* properly set up? Do you have the proper personnel to provide Branchisees with the "backup" they need? Are you equipped to service them efficiently in production and distribution? Are you in a position to fill orders promptly? Your inability to do so can quickly shatter your Branchise program.

Another example of the imperative need of the Branchisor's home office to maximize its efficiency is that of a record shop. In commencing his program, the Branchisor was appalled to realize that it would require at least $100,000 in inventory to properly equip each store, a sum that was much too high for the mom-and-pop Branchisees he was seeking. Analyzing the situation, he realized that such a large inventory was needed because his distribution methods were completely out of date; hence it would take weeks and often months before the Branchisee received replacement stock. Thus a Branchisee tended to overload himself with merchandise to make sure that he didn't run short. The Branchisor solved this by computerizing his distribution procedures: Reorders could now be dispatched the same day as received. Hence a Branchisee could now "get by" with as little as $25,000 in inventory and, yet, be able to offer the same assortment of merchandise as a store with $100,000 in inventory. Thus by "cleaning their own house," the Branchisor was able to convert a nonfeasible program into a feasible one.

This same Branchisor, to further reduce the need for extensive inventory, also established a catalog corner in the store of each Branchisee. These catalogs included some 200 pages and 15,000 products, a total merchandise inventory exceeding $300,000. Thus with only a $25,000 inventory, it was nevertheless able to show and sell merchandise totaling $400,000. No competition was able to equal this. The Branchisee was able to multiply sales potential but keep the same overhead.

Preopening Procedures

TIMETABLE

The responsibility of opening a new business; training personnel; obtaining all necessary equipment, furnishings, supplies and stock; and many other details places a great demand on time and energy. It is therefore important not to overlook any important items which would prevent a smooth and timely opening. Everything possible should be accomplished to bring the operation up to full-operating efficiency prior to the opening.

The purpose of the timetable (Figure 10-1) is to present a "bird's eye view" of this task, showing the major items in relation to time and to each other. The primary

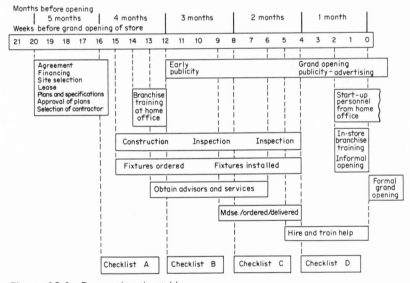

Figure 10-1 Preopening timetable.

advantage of such a timetable is that it prevents overlapping that would result in conflict and puts the priorities where they belong. It is, at best, a guide. It has flexibility and can be adjusted and added to for accommodating special circumstances.

CHECKLISTS

The timetable refers to a series of checklists (A, B, C, D), to be completed at various intervals prior to opening. These checklists include all the items that appear on the timetable plus other items too numerous to be listed. (See pages 157–158.)

CHECKLIST A

To be done 3 to 4 months prior to grand opening.

_____ Approval of construction plans by various municipal departments.

_____ Construction begins.

_____ Two weeks' franchisee training at home office.

_____ Fixtures and equipment ordered by home office.

_____ Contact post office for exact mail address.

_____ Obtain advisory services.

_____ Preliminary arrangements for essential services and utilities.

_____ Register name.

_____ Establish bank account.

_____ Apply for necessary licenses.

_____ Construction progress inspection.

_____ Select insurance program.

_____ Arrange for security service.

CHECKLIST B

To be done 2 to 3 months prior to grand opening.

_____ Construction continues.

_____ Release early publicity announcing appointment as franchisee and construction of store. Find form for this story in this manual. See chapter on *Promotions.*

_____ Put "Coming Soon" sign in window. See "Sales Promotion" section of *Operations Manual.*

_____ Fixtures start arriving.

_____ Check on services and utilities.

_____ Inventory is ordered by home office. List furnished to you.

_____ Obtain legally required inspections (municipal).

_____ Check floor-covering installation date with contractor to be ready for installation of equipment.

_____ Obtain IRS forms, schedules, and withholding permits.

_____ Obtain employment wage and hour regulation sheets, workers' compensation notices, etc., for posting.

_____ Join selected local organizations, including chamber of commerce and Better Business Bureau.

CHECKLIST C

To be done 1 to 2 months prior to grand opening.

_____ Inventory starts arriving.

_____ Check incoming merchandise against shipping lists. Notify home office and supplier of shortages and damage by registered mail.

_____ Begin to stock shelves in accordance with layout and plans given to you by home office.

_____ Check on sales tax permits.

_____ Arrange balance of services, such as laundry, trash disposal, window cleaning, etc.

_____ Frame permits and licenses. Display same.

_____ Start to hire, bond, and train appropriate personnel. See "Administration" section in *Operations Manual.*

_____ Establish list of sources of emergency repair—plumbing, air conditioning, etc.

CHECKLIST D

To be done during 30-day period before grand opening.

_____ Home office training director or field supervisor arrives to give you "start-up" assistance, and to stay with you up to and through your grand opening.

_____ Two weeks of in-store Branchisee training.

_____ Informal opening (unadvertised). Start 10-day dry run before grand opening.

_____ Put "Now Open" sign in window.

_____ Continue employee training as needed.

_____ Check on housekeeping, have windows washed.

_____ Study your grand-opening program in "Sales Promotion" section of the manual

_____ Put grand-opening program into effect.

_____ Formal grand-opening ceremonies.

PROMOTION AND ADVERTISING IN PREOPENING AND GRAND OPENING

The Branchisee just starting out in his new restaurant will need certain selling tools to apprise his local community of his existence and induce people to try him out. He cannot afford to depend upon traffic alone. There are certain basic "actions" that include a preopening and grand-opening promotion. These can be prepared by the Branchisor organization and incorporated into a Branchisee operations manual. Some of these are:

Publicity Release. Such a release is to be placed in newspapers in the Branchisee's territory, shortly after the contract is signed, announcing the appointment of Mr._____ as a Branchisee. The Branchisor organization will submit a representative story which will contain suggested information.

Signs. As soon as the store site is leased, signs should be prominently displayed on the Branchise structure announcing the impending opening of a restaurant. The copy and designs for the signs should be included in the grand-opening package.

About two weeks prior to the opening, signs should be placed in the window over the existing announcement, fixing the date of the grand opening and advertising door prizes, specials, giveaways, etc. Celebrities attending the opening should be highlighted.

Newspaper Ads. Five days prior to the grand opening, an ad should be placed in appropriate newspapers announcing the forthcoming opening.

The newspaper ad for the grand opening should be approximately one-quarter of a page in size and should feature basic "specials." This ad might also anounce drawings for door prizes (if legal in that area).

Decorations. The day before the grand opening, the restaurant should be decorated with grand-opening banners and pennants which may be rented locally by the Branchisee. This decorative material should be left up for a week.

Young People. You might want to recruit students from the local high school to give out free door prizes or coupons in and around the restaurant during the opening week. You might consider having them wear "old-fashioned" apparel.

Local Clubs. Invite these groups for the grand opening, and include local political club officers, church officials, youth organization leaders, etc. Personalized invitations should be sent to them. These personages represent "influence leaders" in a community.

Handbills. Place these under windshield wipers of parked autos in the community; also, put them along industrial parking lots, announcing "grand opening."

Itinerant Clown. This type of promotion has been used with fine results. A clown moves around town, performs his antics, attracts passerby children, etc., and hands out announcements about "family specials" offered during the grand-opening event.

"Teaser" Ads.   A good idea is to place a series of attention-provoking "teaser" ads (small-space ads) in local newspapers announcing the impending opening.

Treasure Chest.   A "treasure chest" is placed in the restaurant, and a key is given with each purchase. "Lucky" keys that open the chest win prizes. This entire project can be inexpensively purchased: It costs about $60 for a chest, prizes, and a thousand keys.

Pre-vue Party.   This idea can be especially effective in small towns. The press and important local luminaries are invited—during opening day—for a pre-vue party with free refreshments provided. It has been our experience that, particularly in smaller communities, even the mayor can be induced to attend—and abundant publicity is thereby obtained.

Radio Spot Announcements.   This is quite inexpensive in most smaller communities and should be considered for Branchisees, particularly during the grand opening.

Roving Vehicle.   This can be an antique auto with eye-catching decorations. It will carry signs about the opening, and the driver will wear a "colonial motif" hat and shirt and will distribute "get-acquainted coupons," e.g., offering free desserts. The auto, parked in front of the restaurant, also doubles as a stationary billboard.

OPERATIONS MANUAL

The operations manual should cover in detail all the necessary training areas and should be designed to be the textbook during the training period at the home office. It should also serve as a permanent ready reference for the branch operator to give him the necessary guidelines for the proper operation of his business. It should cover the administrative aspects of the operation as well as the merchandising methods to be used for best results.

The entire operations manual should be specifically designed as a tool to be used in the running of the operator's business. It should be in loose-leaf form; this allows additions and deletions to be made as they become necessary and allows his "Bible" to be kept up to date, keeping pace with the changes in merchandising and promotion.

It should contain all the necessary procedures and other substantive instruction. It should "spell out" a complete program of personnel management from the hiring of employees to specific job qualifications and responsibilities. The manual should contain the specifics on all subjects covered in the training period, in addition to promotional material for the Branchisee's local use. A sample manual follows.

Outline for
Store Operations Manual

SECTION A—Introduction

- Foreword
- Company history
- The people behind you
- Company's obligation to you
- Franchisee's obligation

SECTION B—Preopening Procedures

- Timetable, from agreement to grand opening
- Receiving fixtures and inventory
- Obtaining advisory services
- Obtaining insurance program
- Obtaining licenses and permits
- Obtaining utilities and other services
- Trade publications and reference books suggested
- Checklists of actions to take:
  3 to 4 months before opening
  2 to 3 months before opening
  1 to 2 months before opening
  Within 30 days before opening

SECTION C—Store Policies

- Image
- Quality standards of products
- Price policy
- Brand policy
- Service and courtesy

- Delivery to customers
- Customer credit
- Check cashing
- Complaints and refunds
- Guarantees
- Maintainence
- Relationship with community
- Store hours
- Employee discounts

SECTION D—Store Routine and Housekeeping

- General housekeeping
- Basic duties of personnel: store manager, clerks, etc.
- Daily store-opening procedure, checklists
- Daily store-closing procedure, checklists
- Checking out register and daily report
- Maintenance of store and equipment
- Self-inspection

SECTION E—Sales Routine

- Order-taking procedure (writing up order)
- Operating cash register
- Making change
- Sales taxes

- Charge account procedure (if applicable)
- Mail-order procedure (if applicable)
- Exchange, adjustments, and refunds (procedure)
- Bags and packages
- Want book

SECTION F—Supplies and Inventory

- Initial orders, showing supply source and initial quantity (by category and item)
- Purchase order forms; how to use for new orders
- Checking in shipments
- Payment
- Pricing procedures
- Taking inventory; procedures and forms
- Inventory control and order-planning guide, form showing minimum quantities (item by item); how much to build to when minimum is reached, etc.
- Preventing losses (through poor records, pilferage, shoplifting)

SECTION G—Administration

- Personnel
    Job chart
    Hiring, qualifications, interviewing
    Application form, checking references
    Hours, shifts, timekeeping
    Vacations, sick pay, time off
    Employee discounts
    Payroll taxes; laws concerning employees
    Rules of conduct for employees
    Training
- Field supervisor's inspection
- Communications and reports (forms to use):
    Between stores and home office
    Between stores and warehouse
    Recurring reports to home office
- Record-keeping and accounting

SECTION H—Sales Promotion

- Grand-opening promotion plans with timetable
- General promotion
    Newspaper
    Radio
    Direct mail
- Seasonal events, major holidays, etc.
- Displays

Housekeeping and Maintenance Frequency Chart

Items to be done daily	Clean grill
	Clean orange juice squeezer
	Clean counter and underneath
	Clean coffee urn
	Clean mustard and other containers
	Empty all trash
	Wipe inside, front, and back of coolers
	Clean refrigerator inside and out
	Clean signs
	Mop floor
	Wipe surface in front of counter and around coolers
	General outside cleaning
	Spray for roaches if necessary
Items to be done weekly	Wash all windows inside and out
	Scrape gum from floor and under counter
	Clean all ornaments
	Wash outside thoroughly
	Check outside sign
	Check all light bulbs
	Clean spouts of coolers
	Clean coffee urns with cleanser
	Check trash cans for cleanliness
Items to be done monthly	Clean filter to exhaust fan
	Clean off grease from exhaust
	Wash interior walls
	Check gas jets—if flame is not high or wrong color, call gas company or grill maintenance
	Wipe dust from cooler motors
	Exterminator service (oftener if necessary)
Items to be done every 6 months	Oil the motors to front coolers
	Take down oranges on the ceiling and clean
	Check and touch up signs if needed
	Vacuum grass on walls
	Have floor professionally cleaned and waxed
Items to be done yearly	Redecorate as necessary
	Maintain signs
	Replace ornaments as needed
	Spray-paint grass on walls

PROPER RECORD-KEEPING

Most small businesses shun contact with the "arithmetic" of their operation—that is, until circumstances *compel them* to use it. At this point, however, it may be too late; the damage may already have been done.

A good record-keeping system should provide an awareness of the day-to-day progress and an understanding of the "break-even point" of business. It gives an insight into comparative ratios of similar businesses to determine relationships; for example, whether they are paying too much money for similar items such as rent, advertising, or personnel salaries. Also, record-keeping creates an awareness of how each department of the operation is doing, enabling one to pinpoint "weak" products or services that should be eliminated.

Temporarily, the arithmetic of a business can be "shoved under a carpet." But at the stage when it does confront you, it may do so in an "explosive" manner:

1. While thinking that you are operating at a profit—with long hours of drudgery to document this—you are actually operating at a loss.
2. You are not in proper control of what you are doing.
3. You may be overpaying for certain things. In many instances these expenditures may be cut in half without impeding your business progress, for example, rent, personnel, advertising, etc.
4. You may be underpaying for certain things that can help to expedite business expansion.
5. You may be overinventoried or underinventoried (both of which can prove damaging to your business status).
6. You may be underpaying on taxes (subjecting you to severe penalties), or you may be overpaying these taxes (again throttling your business progress and earnings potential).
7. You may have a series of wasteful "leakages" in your business, enough of them to "sink your ship" to the extent that it can never be salvaged.

In referring to the arithmetic aspect of your business, we are referring to *record-keeping,* the way you maintain your books and the day-by-day awareness you have of your business activities and status.

Proper record-keeping is vital to the business health of the owner of a small business; even the U.S. Department of Commerce indicated that over 50 percent of small business failures can be attributed to inadequate record-keeping systems.

Accuracy in your figures is also of the utmost importance for other reasons, such as (1) your federal and state tax returns, including income tax and Social Security and (2) your applications for credit from suppliers, manufacturers of equipment, or a bank.

Even more important, your financial statements (profit and loss) about your business give you the figures you must have to know which way your business is going and to help you achieve increased profits. With an adequate record-keeping system, no matter how simple, you can answer such questions as the following:

1. How much business am I doing?
2. What are my expenses? Are any of them running too high?
3. What is my percentage of gross profit or net profit?
4. How much cash do I have in the till, and how much in the bank?
5. What are my collections on charge business?
6. What is the condition of my working capital?
7. How much do I owe to my suppliers?
8. What are the trends in my cash receipts, my expenses, my profits, and my net worth?
9. What is my actual net worth? In other words, what is the value of my owning the business?
10. What is the relationship of my assets to my debts? What percentage am I earning on my investment?
11. How many cents of net profit am I making on every dollar of sales?
12. Is my financial position growing better or worse?

The answers to the above questions are, in effect, danger signals. They tell the owner of a small business where he is going and whether he should do something to change the direction and course of the business. Once he understands the conditions which exist, the Branchisee can take the necessary actions to improve his position.

Whatever system you decide upon should enable you to keep your eye not only on sales, expenses, and net profit but on the balance sheet that tells how much money you owe and discloses the net worth of your business.

Computing Net Worth and Net Profit

Here is how net worth is computed. First you list what you *own,* then what you *owe.* The formula is as follows:

$$Assets - liabilities = net\ worth$$

First total your *assets,* which are your cash on hand, cash on deposit with your bank, merchandise, equipment, business property, accounts receivable, and everything else your business owns. Then subtract your *liabilities,* which are your accounts payable, taxes, notes payable, and everything you owe for either merchandise, equipment, or services. This difference is your *net worth.*

To verify that figure, you can check it by the following method: Take *your net worth at the start of the period* and add to it your *increased capital,* including such items as additional cash put into the business, value of new equipment, etc., invested during this period. Then subtract your *withdrawals,* whether in cash or personal salary. This equals *your net worth at the end of the period.*

If your records are being kept correctly, your net worth as determined by both methods should tally. The following table gives an example of the first method:

Assets:		
Cash on hand	$ 500	
Cash on deposit	3,500	
Merchandise inventory	12,500	
Equipment	3,800	
Accounts receivable	1,900	
		$22,200
Liabilities		
Accounts payable	$ 3,700	
Notes payable	2,200	
Payroll taxes	225	
		−6,125
Net worth		$16,075

Now, let us see how "net profit" would be computed:

Sales (or gross income)	$2,400
Cost of sales	−850
Gross profit	$1,550
Expenses	−680
Net Profit	$ 870

Cost of sales in any business which handles merchandise is generally computed by adding together the opening inventory plus purchases for the period and then subtracting the closing inventory. The closing inventory is calculated on the basis of wholesale price, market value, or cost to you, whichever is lowest.

Operating Ratios

Next, it is important that you have an understanding and awareness of the "operating ratios" pertaining to your particular line of business. Operating ratios are the figures from your profit and loss statement translated into percentages. This gives you a quick, visual conception of "how you're doing." It also exposes areas where you are spending too much—or too little. Most important, it gives you a solid basis for comparing the expenses and income of your business with the ratios of similar businesses. Thus you can establish whether you are doing very well, fairly well, or poorly, in relation to what you *should* be doing in your particular enterprise.

Comparative ratios (pertaining to most types of businesses) are available from Dun

& Bradstreet or the Small Business Association, Washington, D.C. They are also available from specialized sources (pertaining to specific businesses), usually trade magazines for each specific field.

In analyzing your own ratios, keep in mind that there are two types: (1) the ratio of *fixed expenses* (those expenses that generally remain the same month after month) and (2) your *variable expenses* (those that fluctuate from month to month depending on the amount of business you do). A typical ratio analysis would contain these categories shown in the table below. It is a typical ratio analysis pertaining to an automotive store:

Sales		100.00%
Cost of sales		−71.01
Gross profit		28.99
Variable expenses:		
Outside labor	.47%	
Operating supplies	1.18	
Gross wages	8.69	
Repairs and maintenance	.53	
Advertising	1.11	
Car and delivery	.93	
Bad debts	.10	
Administrative and legal	.49	
Miscellaneous expense	.94	
Total variable expenses		14.44%
Fixed expense:		
Rent	1.46	
Utilities	1.29	
Insurance	.86	
Taxes and licenses	.61	
Interest	.37	
Depreciation	1.20	
Total fixed expenses		5.79
Total expenses		−20.23
Net profit		8.76

The Successful Record-Keeping System

Basic requisites for a successful record-keeping system are:

1. It should be simple.
2. It should be easily and quickly usable.
3. It should provide easy procedures for day-by-day figure compilation.
4. It should provide a periodic "summary" enabling an at-a-glance perspective of your business.
5. It should require minimal time on your part (for example, 15 to 30 minutes) to transcribe pertinent figures, usually during the evening.

6. It should be so simple that you can control the system irrespective of any professional accountant you may use.

Fortunately for the owner of a small business, a number of such simplified systems are available enabling quick transcription, easy awareness, and continuing control of business "arithmetic." In most instances these services will also—as part of their overall program for owners of small businesses—go so far as to also prepare tax statements (federal, state, and local). This would include related data, estimates of income, Social Security figures, and a profit and loss statement. All this, at moderate cost, is geared to the limited budgets of small businesses.

A record-keeping system of this type enables precise tax compilation. Most important, it acts to avoid costly overpayments on taxes, and it is estimated that six out of ten owners of small businesses overpay their taxes. In addition to providing these all-important advantages, an effective record system also provides certain "fringe benefits." For example, a merchant who seeks a loan will need an accurate balance sheet to present to the bank; a good set of records can provide such a statement quickly and accurately.

Examples of simplified record-keeping forms are shown in Figures 10-2 to 10-7. They were prepared by and are presented here courtesy of General Business Services, Inc., 51 Monroe Street, Rockville, Maryland 20850.

In examining these forms you'll note the simplicity of the day-by-day business entries, the all-inclusive "pictures" they give you of your business status, and the quickness with which the entries can be made.

To sum up: To assure yourself that you are operating your business successfully and to achieve the kind of earnings you expected when you commenced your business, your maintenance of good records is a "must." It is, in fact, considered every bit as important as sales for the continued good health of your business.

Sales and Income For _December_ 19___

DATE	DAY	1. MONEY RECEIVED FROM CUSTOMERS	2. Deposits	3. TOTAL SALES	4. Sales Tax 3%	5. ITEM A	6. ITEM B	7.	8.
1	TUES	344 04	344 04	386 50	11 59	143 16	231 75		
2	WED	340 12	286 15	405 21	12 15	181 81	211 25		
3	THUR	376 15	310 36	328 02	9 84	108 25	209 93		
4	FRI	415 55	415 55	396 76	11 90	125 16	259 70		
5	SAT	473 77	414 17	408 15	12 24	155 51	240 40		
6	SUN		T 1,770 27						
7	MON	353 28	340 56	385 81	11 57	98 57	275 67		
8	TUES	372 40	372 40	416 98	12 50	186 21	218 27		
9	WED	411 51	208 16	415 77	12 47	178 22	225 08		
10	THUR	360 96	315 83	398 16	11 94	163 80	222 42		
11	FRI	387 36	251 59	378 18	11 34	106 51	260 33		
12	SAT	379 83	362 08	421 21	12 63	185 50	223 08		
13	SUN		T 1,850 62						
14	MON	469 68	193 17	376 12	11 28	140 47	224 37		
15	TUES	398 41	181 81	456 18	13 68	158 32	284 18		
16	WED	387 20	231 75	421 72	12 65	176 57	232 50		
17	THUR	383 12	183 56	385 55	11 56	137 48	236 51		
18	FRI	404 55	391 18	374 41	11 23	187 00	176 18		
19	SAT	360 60	360 60	401 02	12 03	159 16	229 83		
20	SUN		T 1,542 07						
21	MON	439 70	315 14	399 84	11 99	122 49	265 36		
22	TUES	379 95	328 78	402 13	12 06	177 08	212 99		
23	WED	384 15	318 17	371 82	11 15	156 27	204 40		
24	THUR	408 60	400 14	412 10	12 36	182 14	217 60		
25	FRI	Christmas							
26	SAT	389 10	178 18	356 15	10 68	97 31	248 16		
27	SUN		T 1,540 41						
28	MON	381 90	381 90	365 28	10 95	163 22	191 11		
29	TUES	362 04	216 05	387 92	11 63	155 66	220 63		
30	WED	397 80	397 80	378 91	11 36	185 53	182 02		
31	THUR	310 36	301 96	400 56	12 01	174 45	214 10		
			T 1,297 71						
TOTAL		10,072 13	8,001 08	10,230 46	306 79	4005 85	5,917 82		

Money Received from Other Sources

9. Sale of Equipment: FURNITURE	100 -
10. Money Borrowed for the Business	
11. Other:	
12. Total This Month (items 9, 10, 11)	100 -
13. Total Previous Months (item 14 previous month)	500 -
14. Total Year to Date (item 12 plus 13)	600 -

Accounts Receivable Control

15. Accounts Receivable Due from Customers beginning of Month	1,578 02
16. Add total sales for Month (col. 3)	10,230 46
17. Sub-Total	16,808 48
18. Subtract Money Received from Customers (col. 1)	10,072 13
19. Accounts Receivable Due from Customers End of Month	1,736 35
20. Adjustments: OVERCHARGE	(26 08)
21. Balance carried forward SHOULD EQUAL ACCOUNTS RECEIVABLE SUMMARY SHEET TOTAL	1,710 27

Figure 10-2 © 1978 by General Business Services.

Business Expenses For _December_ 19___

(1a) BUSINESS TAXES ITEM LICENSES			(1b) EMPLOYER'S SHARE SOCIAL SECURITY (FICA)		(2) RENT		(3) REPAIRS AND MAINTENANCE		(4) GROSS EMPLOYEES SALARIES		(5) INSURANCE		(6) PROFESSIONAL FEES	
607	County Lic.	58 40	599	650 -			618	41 50	ENTER MONTHLY TOTALS FROM PAYROLL SUMMARY		626	56 -	604	25 -
619	State Lic.	73 40	(1c) UNEMPLOYMENT				635	36 11	31	1040 -				
TOTAL		131 80	TOTAL		650 -		TOTAL	77 61			TOTAL 56 -		TOTAL 25 -	

(7) COMMISSIONS		(8) INTEREST AND BANK CHARGES		(9) ADVERTISING		(10) AUTO-TRUCK		(11) DUES AND SUBSCRIPTIONS		(12) OFFICE SUPPLIES		(13)
		601	37 -	614	111 17	613	107 11	605	25 -	2	1 85	
				17	10 -	624	33 07	625	12 -	3	5 -	
						1	13 -			18	3 -	
						5	13 -			632	87 06	
						9	13 -					
TOTAL		TOTAL	37 -	TOTAL	121 17	17	13 -	TOTAL	37 -	TOTAL	1040 -	

(14) TELEPHONE		(15) UTILITIES		(16)		AUTO-TRUCK		(17) OPERATING SUPPLIES		(18) TRAVEL	
603	47 50	621	91 47			21	13 -	612	193 59		
		622	123 62			24	13 -	634	6 40		
						28	13 -	636	10 12		
TOTAL	47 50	TOTAL	215 09	TOTAL		TOTAL	231 18	TOTAL		96 91	

(19) LAUNDRY AND UNIFORM		(20) Trading Stamps		(21) ENTERTAINMENT		(22) CONTRACT SERVICES		(23) MISCELLANEOUS ITEM		(24)
1	3 30	602	85 -	11	4 -	617	86 -			
8	3 30					2	5 -			
14	3 30					14	2 -			
22	3 30					18	5 -			
29	3 30					28	2 -			
TOTAL 16 50		TOTAL 85 -		TOTAL 4 -		TOTAL 100 -		TOTAL 210 11		TOTAL

SPECIMEN

Figure 10-3 © 1978 by General Business Services.

Monthly Summary For _December_ 19___ Page 3

WITHDRAWALS & PERSONAL EXPENSES OF PARTNERS OR OWNER

CHECK # OR DATE	J. Jones	CHECK # OR DATE	B. Smith
603	230 -		
611	230 -		
615	230 -		
620	230 -		
633	230 -		

1,150 -	← Total This Month
10,810 -	← Total Previous Months
11,960 -	← Total Year To Date

OTHER PAYMENTS
Loans — Notes — Fixtures — Equipment — Deposits
INTEREST PAYMENTS SHOULD BE ENTERED ON PAGE 2 - ITEM 8

CHECK # OR DATE	ITEM	AMOUNT
601	C.D. Bank	200 -
616	Add. Mach.	100 -
623	Auto	500 -

← Total This Month →		800 -
← Total Previous Months →		2,200 -
← Total Year To Date →		3,000 -

MONTHLY PROOF & BALANCE

TOTAL MONEY AVAILABLE THIS MONTH:

1. Beginning of Month: CASH (Including Receipts not yet deposited in bank)		50 -
CHECK BOOK BALANCE		2,117 82
2. Total received from customers this month (Column 1, Page 1)		10,072 13
3. Money received from other sources (Item 12, Page 1)		100 -
4. Total (Sum of Lines 1, 2, 3)		12,339 95

TOTAL MONEY SPENT THIS MONTH:

5. Total Business Expenses this month	3,181 87	
6. Less: Employees Taxes & other items withheld	258 -	
7. Net Business Expenses		2923 87
8. Total Purchases (For Resale)		5435 76
9. Total other Payments on Loans, Notes, Fixtures & Equipment		800 -
10. Total Withdrawals and Personal Expenses of Partners or Owners		1,150 -
11. Payment of Payroll Deductions Withheld		
Ck. # State W/H Tax		
Ck. # Federal W/H & S. S. Tax	247 -	
Ck. # Other		247 -
12. This Month's Expenditures (Sum of Lines 7-11)		10,556 63
13. Total Money Which Should be Available End of Mo. (Line 4 minus Line 12)		1,783 32
14. Actually Available End of Mo.: CASH (Including Receipts Not Yet Deposited in Bank)	410 36	
CHECK BOOK BALANCE	1,372 96	1,783 32
15. Overage or Shortage — Difference Between 13 and 14		—

PROFIT AND LOSS

ITEMS	TOTAL THIS MONTH	TOTAL PREVIOUS MONTHS	TOTAL YEAR TO DATE	%
BUSINESS INCOME:				
a. Money Received from Customers	10,072 13	115,829 67	125,901 80	100
b.				
c. Purchases (For Resale)	5,435 76	63,809 55	69,245 31	55
d.				
e. GROSS PROFIT (a. minus c.)	4,636 37	52,020 12	56,656 49	45
BUSINESS EXPENSES:				
1a. BUSINESS TAXES, LICENSES	131 80	581 60	713 40	.6
1b. EMPLOYER'S SHARE SOCIAL SECURITY		684 32	684 32	.5
1c. UNEMPLOYMENT		393 12	393 12	.3
2. RENT	650 00	7,150 00	7,800 -	6.2
3. REPAIRS AND MAINTENANCE	77 61	826 39	904 -	.7
4. GROSS EMPLOYEES SALARIES	1,040 -	13,520 -	14,560 -	11.6
5. INSURANCE	56 -	904 -	960 -	.7
6. PROFESSIONAL FEES	25 -	275 -	300 -	.2
7. COMMISSIONS		520 -	520 -	.4
8. INTEREST AND BANK CHARGES	37 -	409 80	446 80	.4
9. ADVERTISING	121 17	1372 97	1,494 14	1.2
10. AUTO - TRUCK	231 18	2,724 38	2,955 56	2.3
11. DUES AND SUBSCRIPTIONS	37 -	338 40	375 40	.3
12. OFFICE SUPPLIES	96 91	1,079 45	1,176 36	.9
13.				
14. TELEPHONE	47 50	486 70	534 20	.4
15. UTILITIES	215 09	2,101 79	2,316 88	1.8
16.				
17. OPERATING SUPPLIES	210 11	2,027 58	2,237 69	1.8
18. TRAVEL		338 20	338 20	.3
19. LAUNDRY AND UNIFORM	16 50	180 90	197 40	.2
20.	85 -	795 -	880 -	.7
21. ENTERTAINMENT	4 -	268 15	272 15	.2
22. CONTRACT SERVICES	100 -	1,340 -	1,440 -	1.1
23. MISCELLANEOUS		49 23	49 23	.1
24.				
f. Total Business Expenses	3,181 87	38,366 98	41,548 85	33
g. NET PROFIT (e. minus f.)	1,454 50	13,653 14	15,107 64	12

Figure 10-4 © *1978 by General Business Services.*

Monthly Summary For _December_   19___   Page 3

WITHDRAWALS & PERSONAL EXPENSES OF PARTNERS OR OWNER

CHECK # OR DATE	J. Jones		CHECK # OR DATE	B. Smith	
603	230	–			
611	230	–			
615	230	–			
620	230	–			
633	230	–			
	1,150	–	◄── Total This Month		
	10,810	–	◄── Total Previous Months		
	11,960	–	◄── Total Year To Date		

OTHER PAYMENTS
Loans — Notes — Fixtures — Equipment — Deposits
INTEREST PAYMENTS SHOULD BE ENTERED ON PAGE 2 - ITEM B

CHECK # OR DATE	ITEM	AMOUNT	
601	C.D. Bank	200	–
616	Add. Mach.	100	–
623	Auto	500	–
	Total This Month	800	–
	Total Previous Months	2,200	–
	Total Year To Date	3,000	–

MONTHLY PROOF & BALANCE

TOTAL MONEY AVAILABLE THIS MONTH:

1. Beginning of Month: CASH (Including Receipts not yet deposited in bank)	50	–	
CHECK BOOK BALANCE	2,117	82	
2. Total received from customers this month (Column 1, Page 1)	10,072	13	
3. Money received from other sources (Item 12, Page 1)	100	–	
4. Total (Sum of Lines 1, 2, 3)	12,339	95	

TOTAL MONEY SPENT THIS MONTH:

5. Total Business Expenses this month	3,181	87			
6. Less: Employees Taxes & other items withheld	258	–			
7. Net Business Expenses			2,923	87	
8. Total Purchases (For Resale)			5,435	76	
9. Total other Payments on Loans, Notes, Fixtures & Equipment			800	–	
10. Total Withdrawals and Personal Expenses of Partners or Owners			1,150	–	
11. Payment of Payroll Deductions Withheld					
Ck. # _____ State W/H Tax					
Ck. # _____ Federal W/H & S. S. Tax	247	–			
Ck. # _____ Other			247	–	
12. This Month's Expenditures (Sum of Lines 7-11)			10,556	63	
13. Total Money Which Should be Available End of Mo. (Line 4 minus Line 12)			1,783	32	
14. Actually Available End of Mo.: CASH (Including Receipts Not Yet Deposited in Bank)	410	36			
CHECK BOOK BALANCE	1,372	96	1,783	32	
15. Overage or Shortage — Difference Between 13 and 14					

PROFIT AND LOSS

ITEMS	TOTAL THIS MONTH		TOTAL PREVIOUS MONTHS		TOTAL YEAR TO DATE		%
BUSINESS INCOME:							
a. Gross Receipts (Over Counter)							100
b. SALES	10,230	46	114,768	56	124,999	02	100
c. Purchases (For Resale)							
d. COST OF GOODS	5,571	25	63,178	21	68,749	46	55
e. GROSS PROFIT (a. minus c.)	4,659	21	51,590	35	56,249	56	45
BUSINESS EXPENSES:							
1a. BUSINESS TAXES, LICENSES	131	80	581	60	713	40	.6
1b. EMPLOYER'S SHARE SOCIAL SECURITY			684	32	684	32	.5
1c. UNEMPLOYMENT			393	12	393	12	.3
2. RENT	650	00	7,150	00	7,800	06	6.2
3. REPAIRS AND MAINTENANCE	77	61	826	39	904	–	.7
4. GROSS EMPLOYEES SALARIES	1,040	–	13,520	–	14,560	–	11.2
5. INSURANCE	56	–	904	–	960	–	.4
6. PROFESSIONAL FEES	25	–	275	–	300	–	.3
7. COMMISSIONS			520	–	520	–	.5
8. INTEREST AND BANK CHARGES	37	–	409	80	446	80	.4
9. ADVERTISING	121	17	1,372	97	1,494	14	1.3
10. AUTO - TRUCK	231	18	2,724	38	2,955	56	2.4
11. DUES AND SUBSCRIPTIONS	37	–	338	40	375	40	.3
12. OFFICE SUPPLIES	96	91	1,079	45	1,176	36	1.0
13.							
14. TELEPHONE	47	50	486	70	534	20	.5
15. UTILITIES	215	09	•2,101	79	2,316	88	1.9
16.							
17. OPERATING SUPPLIES	210	11	2,027	58	2,237	69	1.8
18. TRAVEL			338	20	338	20	.3
19. LAUNDRY AND UNIFORM	16	50	180	90	197	40	.2
20. Trading Stamps	85	–	795	–	880	–	.7
21. ENTERTAINMENT	4	–	268	15	272	15	.2
22. CONTRACT SERVICES	100	–	1,340	–	1,440	–	1.1
23. MISCELLANEOUS			49	23	49	23	.1
24.							
f. Total Business Expenses	3,181	87	38,366	98	41,548	85	33
g. NET PROFIT (e. minus f.)	1,477	34	13,223	37	14,700	71	12

Figure 10-5 © 1978 by General Business Services.

Purchases (For Resale) For _December_ 19___

INCLUDES ALL MATERIALS AND SERVICES BOUGHT FOR RESALE

DATE OR CHECK NUMBER	PAID TO	AMOUNT PAID	ITEM A	ITEM B	DATE OR CHECK NUMBER	PAID TO	AMOUNT PAID	ITEM A	ITEM B
608	Linn Wholesalers	1,483 93	601 14	882 79		(Brought forward from preceding column)	4,952 38	2,000 69	2,951 69
609	Brookfield Inc.	1,286 96	508 73	778 23	21	Various Cash	101 15	101 15	
610	Purdin Distributors	448 68		448 68	22	" "	66 30		66 30
1	Various Cash	99 79	99 79		23	" "	95 54	95 54	
2	" "	78 03	78 03		603	Kay Bros.	78 03	78 03	
3	" "	104 55		104 55	630	H. Jenkins + Co.	93 84		93 84
4	" "	102 34		102 34	638	R. Smith + Son	48 62		48 62
5	" "	85 51		85 51					
6	" "	101 32	101 32						
7	" "	92 31		92 31					
8	" "	76 16	76 16						
9	" "	79 39		79 39					
10	" "	86 36		86 36					
11	" "	98 60	98 60						
12	" "	71 33	71 33						
13	" "	72 25		72 25					
14	" "	98 09	98 09						
15	" "	108 96	108 96						
16	" "	69 87		69 87					
17	" "	71 72		71 72		Total This Month	5,435 76	2,275 31	3,160 45
18	" "	73 95	73 95			Total Previous Months	63,809 55	28,505 63	35,303 92
19	" "	84 49	84 49			Total Year to Date	69,245 31	30,780 94	38,464 37
20	" "	77 69		77 69					

ACCOUNTS PAYABLE CONTROL			COMPUTED COST OF GOODS SOLD	
1	Total Invoices Received in Current Month For Resale Purchases	5,571 26	8	Cash Resale Purchase Payments	5,435 75
2	Add: Accounts Payable for Resale Purchases at Start of Month	850 50	9	Add: Accounts Payable for Resale Purchases at End of Month	986 -
3	Sub Total	6,421 76	10	Sub Total	6,421 75
4	Less: Cash Resale Purchase Payments	5,435 76	11	Less: Accounts Payable for Resale Purchases at Start of Month	850 50
5	Accounts Payable End of Month	986 -	12	TOTAL PURCHASES	5,571 25
6	Adjustments	-	13	Add: Inventory — Start of Month	-
7	Balance Carried Forward (Should equal Accounts Payable Summary Sheet Total)	986 -	14	Sub Total	-
			15	Less: Inventory — End of Month	-
	(Post Line 7 to Line 9 of Computed Cost of Goods Sold)		16	COST OF GOODS SOLD (to page 3, Line D profit and loss)	5,571 25

Figure 10-6 © *1978 by General Business Services.*

Analysis Sheet For _____

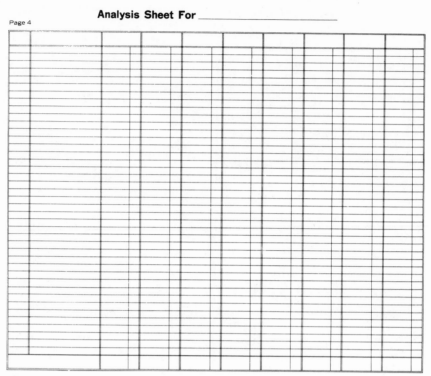

Figure 10-7 © _1978 by General Business Services._

FINDING YOUR "BREAK-EVEN" POINT

You've been working hard serving your customers—so hard that you were sure you had a prosperous year. Yet at the end of the year, you've discovered that instead of a big juicy profit you've made a very small one (or perhaps you've actually incurred a _loss!_).

What's the reason? Perhaps you have failed to keep a tab on the "break-even" point of your business.

What _is_ the break-even point? How do you recognize it?

It's the point in your business operation at which you neither make nor lose money. It means that you have only covered your bare expenses, from which point you need additional sales to bring you a profit.

To phrase it another way, you reach your break-even point when your gross profits equal the sum of your fixed and your controllable expenses.

Let's break this down to simple language. Suppose you are an owner of a small business doing an average business of $3900 a month.

To find _your_ break-even point, do the following:

174   BRANCHISING

1. Decide what your *fixed expenses* are. Fixed expenses are items that remain constant and do not change with the amount of business you do. They include rent, insurance, various taxes you pay, utilities, and depreciation. Let's say that your fixed expenses amount to $600 a month.

2. Write down your maximum sales volume for a month (100 percent of potential volume). This would be $3900.

3. Find your *variable expenses* (expenses that ordinarily increase as your sales increase). These include outside labor, operating supplies, gross wages, repairs and maintenance, advertising, car and delivery, bad debts, administrative and legal expenses, and miscellaneous expenses. Let us assume that you have determined from your records that the average monthly sales can be expected to be about 80 percent of maximum potential ($3100). You will then determine your variable expenses for a $3100 volume. Let us assume that you arrived at $2100 (about 80 percent of $3100).

4. Add your fixed expenses ($600) and your variable expenses ($2100). This gives you a total expense of $2700.

Equipped with these figures, you're now ready to prepare your *break-even chart* (Figure 10-8). This "pictures" the point at which your business has reached a break-even spot under a given set of conditions.

How to Prepare Your Break-Even Chart

1. Draw a blank chart, using Figure 10-8 as a guide. Include equal horizontal divisions, which you will number 0, 10, 20, 30, and so on to 100, representing 0 to 100 percent.

2. Your vertical divisions will, in this example, run from $0 to $3900. We decided

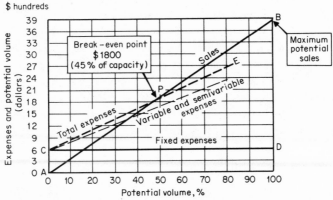

Figure 10-8 Break-even point chart.

to make each vertical division represent $100 in sales, so we numbered the lines 0, 3, 6, 9, and so on to 39. (Any equal division will do.)

3. Rule a line running from $0 to $3900. This would be the line AB in Figure 10-8. Label this "Sales."

4. Rule a horizontal line at $600. This shows your fixed expenses, which stay about the same every month regardless of sales. This is shown as line CD on our chart. Label it "Fixed Expenses."

5. In our example it was determined that the average expected sales would be 80 percent of maximum potential and that "Total Expenses" would be $2700. Run a finger up the vertical line at 80 and another finger across the horizontal line at $2700. Mark a dot, or small x, at the point where these two lines meet. This is shown as point E on our chart.

6. Draw a line from $600 at 0 percent to point E. This is shown as line CE. Label this "Total Expenses."

7. Where lines AB and CE cross each other is your "Break-even Point." This is shown at point P.

8. Point P in our example falls at $1800, which is approximately 45 percent of maximum sales potential. This means that you have to do $1800 worth of business to "break even"—that is, to cover your expenses. You are neither losing money nor making any profit at that point.

What Can a Break-Even Chart Tell You?

- The example above, for instance, tells you that for the particular month in question if you expect to make any profit, it must come from additional sales over and above $1800.
- It can tell you when your sales are not all they should be and signal you to do something about your selling method, your staff, or your merchandise lines.
- It can help you control your budget by telling you what changes you might have to make, if any, to bring expenses in line with income.
- It can tell you how much business you can afford to lose before you are in danger of losing too much. Or, conversely, how profits will increase with sales volume.
- It can tell you what would happen if you were to increase or reduce prices.
- It can tell you if you can afford to raise salaries or whether a reduction in expenses is indicated.
- It can help you appraise your merchandising policy. A break-even chart for each line could tell you which lines should be pushed and which might be eliminated.
- It can tell you in advance if you can afford to make improvements which might affect your expense structure.

Prepare a Break-Even Chart for Each Month

For each month, you should know how much business you must do. Make up your chart *before* the start of the month. For long-range planning, you can make up break-even charts for 6-month or multiyear periods. In this way you will be charting your course to greater and more consistent profits and know where you are going at all times.

Chart's Value Depends upon Good Records

A break-even chart, as a reliable warning system, is only as good as the accuracy of the figures from which it is built. It is of the utmost importance to have a good, simple record-keeping system that accurately reflects sales and expenses day by day. Therefore, actually, the first step in constructing a break-even chart is *to have a good record-keeping system and to keep it in order!* As a user of simplified tax records, you have taken this first important step to the successful use of break-even charts.

UNDERSTANDING YOUR FINANCIAL RATIOS

Today, even though the opportunity for making profits for your business has never been better, there is a great need for basic control of costs and finances in small businesses.

The "ratio" is a proven way to help you judge the financial condition of your business and any financial changes taking place. In most cases, you will be able to see the beginning of any small trouble and stop it before it has a chance to do your business genuine financial harm. The ratio is a "comparison of fractions." This method will show you the relationship between two items: usually between a complete item and one or more parts of it, or between two parts of the same item.

When you apply the percentage ratio to your balance sheet or your profit and loss statement, you can compare items that are part of the same statement or compare various items from different statements. You can use this method to compare your firm with the rest of the industry, for there are standard ratios for all types of businesses.

There are many proven, financial comparisons that can be of valuable use to you as a businessperson. These are listed below, together with examples of their use. In all examples, *use the largest number that will evenly divide each number.*

Current Ratio. This is a comparison between "current assets" and "current liabilities." Current assets are those which will flow into cash during a normal business cycle. They include cash, notes, accounts receivable, inventory, and, at times, short-term and marketable securities listed on the major stock exchanges at easily recognized value.

Current liabilities would include bills due within a short period of time, notes, accounts payable for merchandise, bank loans, and taxes.

If a grocer has current assets totaling $3600 and total current liabilities of $3000, the ratio would be found by doing the following:

$$\frac{3,600}{3,000} = \frac{6}{5}$$

Therefore, his ratio would be 6 to 5, meaning that for every $6 of assets, he has $5 of liabilities.

Operating Ratio. This compares "net profits" to total "net sales."

If a druggist has total net sales of $1800 and the net profit from these sales is $600, the comparison may be as follows:

$$\frac{1,800}{600} = \frac{3}{1}$$

In this example, the ratio would be 3 to 1, or $3 of net sales for every $1 of net profit.

When a comparison of your ratio is made with other firms in the same business, results of ratios of a few years back can be just as useful as the very recent ratios. The most important thing is to get started with a comparison standard.

Earning Ratio. This is the comparison of "total net sales" to "gross earnings."

In the last example, we have assumed that the druggist's total net sales are $1800. If his gross earnings are $1200, this ratio would be:

$$\frac{1,800}{1,200} = \frac{3}{2}$$

This ratio shows that for every $3 of net sales, there are $2 of gross earnings, or a 3 to 2 ratio.

Your cost of goods may affect this as well as other ratios. Costs of goods may seem high simply because of a low selling price. For example, if sales are $10,000 and cost of goods is $8000, then your gross profit on your sales is 20 percent and the cost of goods is 80 percent.

Now, if your gross profit were increased to 25 percent and the cost of goods remained the same, your sales would be $10,666, and the $8000 (cost of goods) would represent only 75 percent of sales.

Unit Cost Ratio. This is the comparison of the "costs of production" and the "physical volume" produced.

If a manufacturer finds that his actual production costs come to $300 for every 1500 cases of merchandise sold, the example would be compared as follows:

$$\frac{1,500}{300} = \frac{5}{1}$$

Therefore, for every 5 cases of merchandise, the manufacturer has production costs of $1. This ratio is 5 to 1.

Capital Employed Ratio.   This one is the comparison showing how much "capital was invested" to produce "net profits."

If the druggist's net profits were $600 and he invested $500 to obtain these profits, the ratio can be figured as follows:

$$\frac{600}{500} = \frac{6}{5}$$

On the basis of this ratio, we find that $6 of profits are received from every $5 of invested capital.

If you compare your ratio to that of another business in the same line and you find that the gross profit should be 25 percent, that does not mean you must average 25 percent gross for every single item you sell. Your competition may force you to lower your profit margin on some items.

However, there may be excellent reasons in your business for your company to be higher or lower than your competitor on certain items or ratios. The main consideration must be that you have a pricing policy which is sound and well balanced.

Fixed Property Ratio.   This is the ratio of "fixed assets" (fixtures, furniture, property, etc.) and "total net sales."

A plumber has fixed assets totaling $3600. His total net sales are $12,000. Therefore, to find how much was invested to produce each dollar of net sales, the ratio would be:

$$\frac{12,000}{3,600} = \frac{10}{3}$$

The plumber finds that $10 of sales were produced for each $3 invested in fixed assets.

The application of the ratio for comparing various items connected with the operation of your business can be most helpful. You will be able to spot any weak points in your business with these comparisons. You can stop "overspending" on a particular item if you find that your sales are not that much greater than what you are spending to produce them. You will be able to readjust any items that you find are becoming too costly in the operation of your business.

Potential Uses for the Ratio

The following headings indicate areas that would benefit from analysis by ratio:

Management Wages.   Owner's compensation is an item worthy of analysis. In a proprietorship or partnership, for instance, it is often the practice to compute profits *before* allowing any compensation to the owner or owners. After all other deductions, whatever earnings are left usually represent the compensation.

Employee Wages and Salaries. Wages and salaries will naturally be the major item among the operating expenses on your profit and loss statement. You will gain much when you know how others in your line are managing these expenses.

Occupancy Costs. Occupancy costs are important to all businesses and, in particular, to retailers. Every dollar paid in rent should bring a proportionate return in income. If your location costs are high in relation to your sales, they should be offset by correspondingly higher prices. Many "exclusive" shops, located on "elegant" avenues and streets, take this principle for granted.

Advertising. Advertising is a powerful factor in attracting customers. Nearly every small business will find it profitable to provide at least part of its expense budget for advertising. Many manufacturers are also finding that the money they spend for advertising is attracting many people to their names, products, and styles.

If you find that your former advertising budget was too low, an increase might bring in more income.

Credit. You will also want to watch out for bad debts. Credit is becoming the rule rather than the exception in all business today. It certainly will "boost" sales, and there is money in it. Firms handling high-priced items find that through credit they are able to maintain high profit margins. In other firms where the markup cannot be increased, a larger volume of business offsets the minor credit risk.

Don't, however, become careless in granting credit. Require credit applications and, as a rule, keep an account's credit within certain predetermined limits. The businessperson who grants credit carelessly is asking for financial trouble.

Summary

The time you take to determine the ratios of your business will be time very well spent, for you will always have an accurate picture of your financial status.

At all times, you will have the information to enable you to operate your business with the best financial efficiency. With all of this information at your fingertips, you will definitely have an edge over your competitors because you are maintaining the financial condition of your business on a current basis.

CREATING AN EFFECTIVE IMAGE

Finally, we must say a few words about the art of salesmanship. Since the objective of a Branchising program is to achieve success on the local level, we offer the following advice to local entrepreneurs about creating an effective sales image:

Thirty-Six Ways to Make People Do Business with You, and You Only

It happens in every community. You see two stores. They sell the same merchandise and charge the same prices. They are as identical as two peas in a pod. But one store is empty, and the other is full. It is crowded with customers and is prospering. How do we account for the difference in business?

The same is true of people. They appear alike. Many seem to have the same degree of ability. Yet some people succeed in everything they do, and others fail. Why? What is responsible?

It's not really that much of a mystery. I attribute the difference between the winners and the losers, both in businesses and people, to one word: *image.* The word may sound simple but its meaning is not. Image is intangible in some ways but tangible in many others. It is essentially the collective impression created in the mind of the viewer. The successful enterprise has an image that appeals to customers and stimulates their patronage. The unsuccessful one has an aura of failure about it.

It is the same with people. Everybody likes the image of a winner. They sense it and respond to it. On the other hand, the losers have quite the opposite image. People see their indecision, irresolution, and aimlessness and tend to avoid them.

Never forget that the kind of image you create makes the difference between a prospective customer buying from you and his buying from a competitor; it's the difference between eager, constant, repeat business and the casual, occasional sales.

But how do you get it? How does one create an aura of success? How does one build good will? Why do some businesses have it? Why not others? Why do some people have it? Why not others? Good will results from a favorable image, an image that radiates from a business. It sets your enterprise apart from your competitors. It is a place people want to do business with—again and again.

Central to any favorable image is the determination to succeed. If you tell yourself you won't succeed, you never will. If you tell yourself you will succeed, it is almost a foregone conclusion that you will. It is as simple as that. Create the proper image in your mind's eye that you wish to attain. Eventually that image will come through, not only to you but to others. It isn't something you can build overnight. You have to work at it, but it is worth everything you put into it.

A significant aspect of having a favorable image is the manner in which you conduct yourself with customers. In the give and take of daily life, you make judgments about your customers. They make judgments about you. You create impressions which, when you add them up, become an image.

We have thirty-six ideas to offer that will assist you in building a favorable image. Study these ideas. Apply them. They will mean money in your pocket and orders on your books. They will make the difference between repeat business and one-time buying. They will make people want to do business with you and you only.

1. Remember Names and Places.   Ever meet a business acquaintance after a long period of separation? He smiled, grabbed you by the hand, and greeted you by name.

Weren't you impressed? On the other hand, if someone you know forgets your name, it's not very flattering. The odds are in favor of a negative result. Remembering names is good for your image. Try to develop the habit—it will pay dividends.

2. Be a Joiner.   Socializing, mixing, and mingling with people can be fun. It gets you out of yourself. It broadens you. More important, it is good business to join clubs and organizations in your town. It not only allows you to help others and be a good citizen, it helps you know people who can help you and your business. The contacts you make can be useful at some future time.

3. Be a Good Listener.   We all have problems. We are partial toward those who are willing to listen to them. Besides, everyone likes to hear himself talk, and he likes the people who let him sound off. If you listen, you'll get to know people better. It is your way of showing your interest in them and not only for the immediate transaction. If you listen when they talk, they will listen when you talk.

4. Play up the "You" Appeal.   If you want the customer's business, show him how you serve *his* needs. If you are selling cupcakes to supermarkets, make sure you tell them about your new packaging material which gives them a longer shelf life. This way of selling has come to be known as the marketing orientation. Though well-known in the consumer field, it is not embraced by heavy industry. It demands that you really get to know your customer's business, and it gives you a great advantage.

5. Be Helpful.   There's a great deal to be said for those who help us without grinding their ax. There are hundreds of ways to demonstrate your interest in the welfare of your business contacts, aside from your desire to sell to them. For instance, one salesperson clipped news of importance to clients and sent the clippings along. If you pick up information in your travels, you can pass it along. You are doing something for them. They won't forget it, and they will probably think of doing something extra for you.

6. Demonstrate Your Integrity.   Let people know that you keep your word. Live up to the promises you make. Over the long run it is a policy that pays off. The public is not inclined to tolerate shoddy goods or broken promises from business people, and businesspeople, in turn, want more than goods from their suppliers. Integrity is an important quality to have. Your reputation for integrity will spread quickly through the trade by word of mouth and will pay off in business referrals.

7. Be Consistent.   In the prices you quote and in the claims you make, don't tell one customer one thing and another customer something else. I know an appliance dealer who gave three customers three different prices in a 1-week period for a stereo set. Unfortunately, these customers were members of the same health club. They compared notes and he lost all three sales. Such inconsistencies cause serious damage to your image.

8. Give Service.   Special attention and personalized service are appreciated. This extra interest will pay off in additional business. Take the case of Frank Murphy, a vacuum cleaner salesman I know. He turned a disaster into a triumph. One day, by accident, he stopped at a house where a homemaker had purchased a vacuum cleaner from another salesperson in his company. He was shocked when his friendly approach was met with a storm of abuse. The machine had not been used because of a mechanical defect. Frank brought it back to his firm and had it repaired. The service he performed for this woman made her a permanent friend of the company and brought him several new customers by referral.

9. Be Creative.   Keep thinking up new benefits that your customer can derive through your product or service. Think of your customer's special problems and how your product or service can help in relation to them. A manufacturer of women's panty hose became a multimillion-dollar organization, the foremost in the world, in its field through creativity. For instance, beautiful trees of multicolored ice-cream cones were devised which had panty hose encased within the plasticized cones. These trees were displayed in hundreds of stores throughout the country. Panty hose was also placed in plasticized baseballs that were distributed in ballparks as Mother's Day gifts. They were also placed in fishbowls so that the customer could buy on impulse. And there were many other innovations that helped to provide this company with literally thousands of new customers eager to buy the product.

10. Be Systematic.   Organization, planning, and systems can make things far easier for you. The old exhortation "plan your day and work your plan" is more true today than ever. If selling is involved, prearrange the coverage of your territory from day to day and plan your contacts so as to cover the maximum number of prospects. A map is very helpful. To target the map, use colored pins: red for customers, black for prospects, and green for suspects. Then based on the number of calls you can make each day, estimate the amount of time needed to cover the entire territory. Subdivide your territory into areas in such a way that you can make a maximum number of calls with a minimum of travel. Your adopting this system means a gain in productivity that is certain to benefit you.

11. Be Self-Motivating.   Business is a school of constant hard knocks: So many things can go wrong. Don't let adversity wrestle you to the mat. Take a positive attitude toward it. Remember the sun shines most brilliantly after a heavy shower. I remember a hardware jobber who had the largest order in his history for portable hand tools. Suddenly his supplier had a strike and couldn't deliver. My friend was fit to be tied. He was very depressed, but then his natural bounce asserted itself. He went out and found another supplier. And to top it off, his new source sold him the product for less than the old one. View setbacks in their proper perspective, and set your business course with conviction and determination.

12. Be Affirmative—Not Negative.   Nobody likes a knocker. There's no sound reason for it. Elaboration on the deficiencies of a rival product invites suspicion. Instead, elaborate on what *you* and *your product* can do. You'll be more believable. When one knocks a competitive product—even though it may be true—there's a tendency for the listener to attribute your remarks to "sour grapes," rather than give credence to it.

13. Be Thoughtful and Considerate. A friendly relationship with your customers will take you a long way. The best way to have it is through a genuine interest in them. A follow-up thank-you note, a birthday remembrance, or an occasional friendly phone call can create good will at little cost in money or time. It broadens the entire relationship. Thoughtfulness of this kind not only will bring dividends but will give you personal satisfaction.

14. Be Alert. Watch for new ideas and developments in your field. Read the major business publications and the trade press. Find out what your competitors are doing. Think about how to improve your products and services by incorporating a new material, a new way of doing things, or a new process. Most of all, see how these ideas can be turned to the advantage of your customers.

15. Be Neat. A businessperson makes his best impression when he's dressed in a fairly conventional manner. Wearing expensive jewelry, race-track-type neckwear, or sports shirts can turn off many customers. Businesspeople like to deal with people who take their business seriously. Also pay attention to the details of your daily dress: avoid a tie that is ever so slightly stained or a suit that is losing its press. The same is true of the presentations you offer. Nothing can be more discouraging or harmful to sales than crumpled or soiled pages included in your presentation material.

16. Be Patient. Remember that potential customers don't know your product or service as well as you do. What you may consider elementary may appear complex to them. Develop your sales pitch in "stages" with numerous valid reasons "why," which are to be absorbed and digested a little at a time. Also, be patient with people who work for you. Often employees need a little careful cultivation to turn out well. And be patient with yourself—don't be your own worst critic. Give yourself the benefit of the doubt.

17. Be Logical. Appealing to your prospect's intelligence can often carry you far. It is a firm foundation on which to build. We all know the salesperson who depends only on emotion to sell. And we all know that too many of his orders are canceled when the prospect has second thoughts. Make your approach believable, and avoid evasive answers to your customer's questions.

18. Be Specific. Avoid generalities. Whenever and wherever possible give specific figures and supply documentation to prove your point. Most businesspeople, particularly the successful ones, are hardheaded. They want and respect facts. You must be specific to do business with them.

19. Be Authoritative. You must be the expert; you must display the expertise needed to carry the day. You must read up on all the instruction material and, moreover, understand it so that you can explain it clearly to prospects. You must thoroughly familiarize yourself with your products. In this way you can speak with confidence, the customers can depend on you, and you can gain their respect and loyalty.

20. Show Humility. Though you should always maintain your aura of authority, there will be times when you haven't the answer. When this happens, admit it frankly instead of trying to bluff your way through. In such cases, merely say, "I don't know, but we have highly paid experts in our company. I'll be glad to consult them for the answer." Honesty and humility are things to be respected in any business relationship.

21. Be Generous. It is too easy to find fault with other people. Most often these faults are the faults of our own personalities. Look for the good points, not the bad ones. You'll find you get on better with people. Be generous, too, with small attentions that show genuine interest. Treating the prospect to lunch will be appreciated. It will help each of you to know each other better. It will take a business arrangement and move it on to a new plane of friendship.

22. Be Punctual. Keep your appointments on time. Remember, time is money. Lack of punctuality may be regarded as an insult by your prospect and an indication that you consider your time worth more than his. It is also considered a sign that you do not take your business engagements seriously enough.

23. Display Good Manners. This may seem elementary, yet it is of vital importance in building a good image. Little things like asking permission to smoke, being considerate of the prospect's time and upcoming appointments, apologizing for outside interruptions, and closing doors softly help establish you as a person with whom it is nice to do business.

24. Be Original. Don't allow yourself to become dull or monotonous with the same sales talk and approach. That way, boredom sets in quickly, not only for your customer but for you too. The customer wonders why he should see you since he already knows your pitch. Constantly analyze yourself: You may find yourself mechanically giving your sales talk. You must seek to dramatize and to give excitement to your endeavors. One of our favorite salesmen, Jed Burton, was having a hard time early in his career. He was selling a very prosaic product: the monkey wrench. Everyone had a wrench; few people felt they needed another. Then he got an idea. He announced proudly to his prospects, "I'm here to sell you 1000 tools for the price of one." This dramatized the product and created new interest in his item. It was another form of the advice of a world famous salesperson: "Sell the sizzle—not the stick."

25. Be Cheerful. Maintain a cheery demeanor. Make every effort to keep your personal troubles out of your business life. Dejection communicates itself and dampens both your sales efforts and your prospects' interest. A ready, sincere smile is another way to impress others with your desire to be friendly. Good cheer has a way of spreading itself to others. It is infectious and reciprocal and encourages people to want to do business with you.

26. Be a Graceful Loser. Even if you don't get the order, show the same amount of cordiality as you did at the outset of your sales effort. Displaying irritation will not only make matters worse but it will ruin your future prospects. Maintaining your equilibrium and being a graceful loser will earn you a measure of respect, and chances are you'll have better luck next time.

27. Be Brief and Time-saving.   As noted earlier, time is an important coin of the business realm. It should not be wasted. Keep your sales pitch and visits as brief as possible. Prospects will highly regard you for it. They will readily welcome you back because they know you are a timesaver, not a time-waster.

28. Don't Be a Lecturer.   A sales meeting shouldn't be a monologue. The most effective ones are two-sided discussions, not one-sided. Make yours conversational, invite your prospect's participation. Develop pauses and questions throughout to stimulate his involvement. In this way, he sells himself by means of his own comments and ideas. A good rule is to let him do more than 50 percent of the talking. Encourage him to ask questions, and answer them patiently.

29. Be an Anticipator.   Before you see your prospect, anticipate the personal factors, the problems, and the questions that may arise. Try to see what you can find out about his nature. Is he the friendly, informal type who likes to discuss things with you? Is he the authoritative type who expects deference and formality from the salesperson? Is he a businesslike person who wants to get to the point quickly? Or is he a prima donna liable to fly off the handle at the least deviation from his viewpoint? This kind of forethought will permit you to handle yourself better with the different kinds of prospects you meet. By anticipating you may also be able to bypass the negative and concentrate on the positive.

30. Be a Note Taker.   For those of us who haven't total recall, taking notes provides an invaluable record which can be referred to in the future. It should include all the key points of any meeting. You can see what did or didn't work. You can set yourself for the prospect's attitudes. You needn't take notes during the meeting itself, but you should make them right after it. And make sure they don't get lost. By taking notes, you will also be able to assure correct follow-through.

31. Be Friendly, but Not Overfamiliar.   There is a fine line between friendship and overfamiliarity. You need to be able to sense when you are overstepping it. So often it will depend on the nature of the person you are doing business with. What will be acceptable to one, will not be to the other. When you are in doubt, fall back to a less "familiar" position. Remember, a prospect may feel pressured by overfamiliarity. It can create resentment that will ruin a deal.

32. Get Fun out of Your Work.   If your work is a boring, deadly, dull grind to you, you'll certainly fail at it. It can't be something that you don't want to do but feel you ought to do and that you have to push yourself to do each day. If you want your prospects to enjoy doing business with you, rather than with your competitor, you have to learn how to enjoy your work. And very often this is merely a question of attitude. Joe Marshall hated selling because he did it badly. Every time he approached a prospect, he anticipated a defeat. After 4 months at it, the company teamed him with one of its better salespeople, Bill Holzman. To Holzman, selling was fun. Marshall couldn't understand it: How could selling be fun? Holzman explained that they were going to meet lots of nice people, going into interesting homes, starting on new adventures, and being paid for it besides. "But what is fun about having the door slammed in your face?'' asked Marshall. His friend said that it meant he had one less person to sell and that made his day all the easier. Marshall got the point, his attitude changed, and he found his work progressively easier. After a while, it became fun for him, too.

33. Display Self-Respect.   Put yourself on an equal level with your customer. He buys your product or service because it is useful and thus valuable, not for any other reason. Moreover, if you wish him to respect you, you must respect yourself. You must be polite but not servile. In this day and age, servility is not considered a virtue.

34. Be Forthright.   Answer all questions fully and fairly—right on the line. Don't give inadequate half-answers. When your prospect realizes you are not trying to duck or to evade issues, he will respect you and that respect will be communicated to your product or service.

35. Exercise Polite Persistence.   A turndown is no reason to be deterred from trying again. After a reasonable waiting period, you are free to make a polite renewal of your sales effort. It won't offend the customer and may well bring about a sale. Once again, it becomes a matter of being able to know when persistence becomes offensive because of ill-timed insistence and when persistence is worthwhile.

36. Don't Misuse the Hard Sell.   I'm not suggesting that high-pressure salesmanship is to be entirely avoided. Pressure must always be maintained to see that prospects fully understand the product and that explanations and facts are thoroughly understood as well as benefits. Don't overwhelm the customer with exaggerations, extravagant claims, or by price cutting that cheapens your product. Stick to the facts, and make sure they're well understood. If you do this for qualified prospects, you'll have done all you can to sell him and to maintain good will. You'll be welcomed back the next time, rather than avoided.

Summary

By this time, I hope you have become aware of what goes into creating an image. As you see, you are the artist who paints his own picture. The manner in which you handle yourself, the impression you give, the integrity you display, the consistency, the sincerity, and the planning are but main brush strokes on the canvas. They provide the reason that people want to do business with you and you only. They are your image.

Don't believe that the world has become so mechanical, so computerized, and so impersonal that human beings don't matter in business. The more identical the products become, the more important are those who sell them. Your objective, then, is to build an image which is so positively radiant that it sets you apart from your fellows. Undoubtedly you have been doing some things right. Now go ahead and do the others.

Building an Insurance Plan

Improper insurance—or inadequate insurance—can spell the ruination of a business operation. Any one of a dozen unanticipated mishaps can completely "wipe out" the investment of the businessperson.

Proper and adequate insurance can give all-over protection that means continued security for the businessperson. It can "cushion" him against most mishaps—both business and personal.

In arriving at a formula as to how much insurance you should take for your business, always ask yourself this question: "How much can I *afford to lose* if wiped out by a disaster of any type beyond my control?" Use this simple query as a rule of thumb. For example, if the assessed value of your property is $50,000, can you afford to take only $30,000 in insurance and absorb a potential loss of $20,000?

Another basic thing to keep in mind is that being a businessperson you can't afford to rely on a collection of *individual* insurance policies, each purchased without regard to the other, as part of a basic program. You need an *overall* basic *program*.

Nor can you afford to overinvest in insurance as this, too, can become a ruinous burden. Often (in the interest of insurance economies) you avoid "gambling" on possibilities and invest only in *probabilities.*

There is no set rule as to how much to spend for insurance. This varies with different enterprises, locations, types of stock, and many other factors. The general, small-business average is 1 percent of gross income. Thus, if your anticipated gross for the year is $50,000, you normally would not exceed an expenditure of $500 per year for your insurance coverage.

Your agent or broker is prepared to render valuable assistance by "insurance survey" or "risk analysis" which will produce the facts necessary for intelligent insurance decisions.

The types of business coverages that can save you money are described below. Always keep in mind, *you* are the beneficiary of insurance. As the owner, any

ELEVEN

uninsured losses would come out of your pocket. Fire, windstorm, explosion, or death is each a recognized loss, but hidden and more disastrous losses can occur from interrupted business, terminated leases, or destroyed leases. Any loss means potential *future* damage, as well as immediate damage.

RECOMMENDED COVERAGE

Fire Insurance. Have your property properly appraised so that it is insured for its full insurable value. Be sure that you reexamine your fire insurance periodically to make sure it covers new, current value. Add to your coverage as needed.

It is also advisable that you find out to what extent, if any, the landlord's insurance covers you and then obtain added insurance in the amount you wish.

Inventory Insurance. It is advisable that your inventory insurance be slightly higher than your normal inventory. To protect your periodical "inventory fluctuations," arrange to obtain periodical extended coverage from your insurance broker. Keep an accurate account of inventory so that the exact replacement value is known at all times.

Burglary Insurance. To give yourself maximum coverage, bear in mind that this insurance includes protection against loss resulting from the following crimes:

Burglary. This requires forcible entry. For example, your safe is broken open or a person breaks into your place of business after it is closed (carrying off merchandise or office equipment).

Robbery. Property is taken by violence or the threat of violence.

Theft and larceny. This is the stealing of property while it is unprotected. For example, a person finds the door of your business establishment open, enters, and steals your property.

If you rent a store, a storekeeper's burglary and robbery policy may answer your need. If you operate an office, you may want an office burglary and robbery policy.

Workers' Compensation. This type of insurance protects employees against loss resulting from job-connected accidents or certain types of occupational illnesses. Generally, the employer is compelled by state law to carry this insurance. Premium rates are influenced by the percentage of weekly pay allowed as a benefit. Amounts paid for medical treatment also form an important element of cost. The only way to reduce this insurance expense is to reduce accidents.

Accidents and Health Insurance. This type of insurance helps to reimburse an employee for expenses resulting from an off-the-job injury or a major illness. It also covers the loss of income while the employee is unable to work. A sound health and insurance plan will (1) act as an inducement to prospective employees, (2) help reduce employee turnover, and (3) promote better morale and loyalty to the company (thus increasing productivity).

Use and Occupancy Insurance. Should your business be interrupted or suspended due to serious damage, use and occupancy or earnings insurance will provide you with the same profits as though there were no interruption at all. A total stoppage of business is not necessary to be able to collect. You can also collect on partial shrinkage of business profits resulting from designated damage.

Shrinkage of sales can result from damage by fire, breakdown of machinery, vandalism by striking employees, explosions, broken water pipes, and a variety of other misfortunes.

General Liability Insurance. This type of insurance usually comprises two parts: (1) bodily injury, which covers claims for the accidental injury or death of persons (other than employees) and (2) property damage, which covers accidental injury to the property of others which is not being used by the insured or in his care.

Within the scope of this insurance, the following are most important:

1. Basic coverage. This type of coverage insures liability for accidents occurring on the business premises or arising out of the use of the premises for business purposes. This is ordinarily obtainable through the owners', landlords', and tenants' liability policy. The premium is normally figured on the number of square feet in the area to be insured, with in some cases an additional charge for frontage.

2. Products liability. This covers any dangers arising through the use of products or services, for example, accidents from defective electrical apparatus, poisoning from food or from dyes in textiles, and many miscellaneous hazards.

3. Automobile insurance. There are two principal forms of automobile insurance: (1) automobile liability and (2) automobile physical damage. The first form protects the car owner or operator against damage suits arising from automobile accidents. The second form reimburses the owner for loss of or damage to his own car. There are three types of physical damage insurance within the category of automobile insurance: (1) fire, (2) theft, and (3) collision.

Contractual liability. This type of insurance covers liability imposed by law for negligence.

The most popular type of insurance policy to cover all these areas is the comprehensive general liability policy which provides automatic coverage for many of the new, unanticipated hazards that may develop after you have purchased your policy.

Business Life Insurance. This insurance is a necessary protection for either a business or the family of a businessperson. Uninsured financial loss can occur because of the death of someone associated with the business. It is best to maintain business continuity and your *full value in business* for your family. The main types of coverages are (1) keyperson protection—reimburses the loss upon the death of a key employee; (2) partnership insurance—retires a partner's interest at death; (3) corporation insurance—retires a shareholder's interest at death; (4) proprietorship insurance—provides for maintenance of business upon the death of a sole proprietor; (5) insurance to aid a firm's credit status—covers owner or keyperson during the period of a loan or the duration of a mortgage; and (6) where the estate of a businessperson consists almost entirely of his interest in a business, insurance on his life is payable to his family on his death, providing them with cash and aid in the liquidation of his interest in the business.

Fidelity Insurance. This protects you against losses of property and money because of fraud or dishonesty by one or more employees. Your best coverage could be a "blanket bond" which covers losses resulting from the dishonest act of any employee, regardless of name or position.

INSURANCE CHECKLIST

Here is a helpful insurance checklist to use when reviewing your financial situation with your agent or broker. All the phases of protection may not be required in your business, but it would be well for you to be familiar with all the insurance protection offered:

Buildings

Fire
Improvements and betterments
Extended coverage
Vandalism and malicious mischief
Earthquake and flood
Sprinkler leakage and water damage
Glass
Business interruption (contingent BI in agreed amount)
Extra expense
Rent and leasehold
Replacement cost
Debris removal
Demolition

Business

Keyperson life
Business continuation
Life: Proprietorship, partnership, closed corporation

Employees (Protection of Human Life Values)

Group life
Salary savings
Pension plan, company OASI
Group disability
Medical payment
Workers' compensation
Nonoccupational disability
Unemployment compensation

Liability against Wrongful Actions

Owners, landlords, and tenants
Manufacturers
Contractual
Contingent
Elevator
Comprehensive general

Merchandise

Inland marine
Transportation, parcel post
Salesperson's samples
Exhibition floater
Robbery and safe burglary

Installment sales floater
Ocean marine cargo
Burglary, robbery, and theft
Open stock burglary
Money and securities, 3-D broad form

Equipment

Boiler and machinery
Auto physical damage
Aircraft damage
Marine hull
Auto liability
Nonownership

Neon sign
Use and occupancy

Protection against Human Failure

Honesty, ability, and financial strength
Supply bond
Contract bond
License and permit bond
Schedule position bond
Blanket position bond
Primary commercial blanket bond
Depositors forgery bond

Site Selection

EVALUATION OF MARKETING TERRITORY

The level of demand for a brand-name product or service is rarely the same in diverse geographic locations. For many reasons—including the important one of which company arrived first—the receptivity offered a new Branchisee to a particular area may be more or less than that accorded other Branchisees of the same company. Therefore, a prospective Branchisee must study the trading area in which he expects to sell.

Answers should be sought for the following: Does the proposed territory have enough potential for the product or service; i.e., does it have sufficient ability to buy? Among the facts needed might be total population, population per square mile, population by age, population by ethnic origin, population trends; birth rate, number of families, size of families, marriage rate, death rate; number of homes, number of apartments; income levels, spending habits, bank deposits; ownership of telephones, cars, and major appliances; number of employed and unemployed; and the education levels and various schools.

Is the potential sufficient to produce a level of profit commensurate with the Branchisee's needs?

What are the present buying habits for this kind of product or service?

Does there seem to be a need and desire for your brand of product or service? If necessary, a consumer study should be conducted.

Does the proposed territory constitute a logical, whole trading market or are some parts excluded?

The Branchisee may or may not have an exclusive territory. If he does not, the Branchisor must maintain the confidence and cooperation of the Branchisees by not oversaturating a particular market.

SITE SELECTION

For many Branchise businesses, especially those dependent upon the walk-in or drive-in public, site selection is one of the most crucial operating decisions. Site selection refers not to the territory within which the Branchisee is entitled to operate but to the location, or address, where his business will be established. Branchisors often reserve the right to approve the site. Although the Branchisee usually selects his

TWELVE

own site, the Branchisor often finds a suitable site first and then begins looking for a Branchisee to build on it.

Some of the important factors which must be evaluated when considering potential sites are:

Cost	Neighborhood
Automobile traffic density	Taxes
Safe and convenient entry and exit	Utilities
Pedestrian traffic density	Zoning regulations
Parking facilities	Police and fire service

Information on the use of census data in selecting a site for a business is given in Appendix B.

LOCATION AND SITE PREPARATION CHECKLIST

The following checklist will give you all the concrete data you need for a site selection.

Location and Site Preparation Checklist

1. City _____County _____State _____Population _____
   Common Address of Property_____
   General Location _____

2. Owner _____Address _____
   City _____State _____Phone _____

3. Attorney _____Address _____
   City _____State _____Phone _____
   Realtor _____Address _____
   City _____State _____Phone _____

4. Improved lease _____
   Asking rental _____
   What are taxes with improvements _____
   Will landlord give 20-year lease and options _____

5. Land lease _____Asking rental _____Term _____Tax rate
   _____

6. Purchase_____Asking price _____
   Cash _____Contract _____

7. Street and traffic information
   Main St. & Highway No. _____No. of traffic lanes _____
   Dividers _____Speed limit _____Stop signs & lights_____
   Is street one-way _____Does traffic back up at peak hours _____
   Traffic count, 19____, _____Anticipated highway changes

8. Other area information
   Visibility from both directions _____
   Other eating establishments in the area_____
   Distance away _____Competitive menu _____
   Ethnic background of people within 1 mile _____
   2 miles _____3 miles _____
   Urban renewal planned _____When _____
   Shopping centers planned _____When_____

New housing area planned _____ When _____

9. Distance to business activity

Downtown shopping area _____ Miles _____

Shopping centers (25 stores or more)_____

Number of stores _____ Miles from site _____

Shopping hours

Weekdays _____ Saturday _____ Sunday _____

University _____

Enrollment _____ Regular

Enrollment _____ Summer

High school _____

Enrollment _____

Are students permitted cars _____

Are students permitted to eat off school property _____

10. Land information

Lot size_____ Is it a corner lot _____

Is alley next to property _____ Size _____

Attach plot plan or drawing of property.

Is land at street level_____ If not, give facts below.

11. Zoning data

What type zoning on property _____

Will zoning permit self-service drive-ins _____

Is additional approval required by any planning commission or government_____

12. General site information

Is gas available _____ Is sanitary sewer available _____

How far to hookup _____ Size _____

Will hookup be permitted _____ Is storm sewer available_____

How far from hookup _____

Has storm sewer ever been known to back up _____

Is water service available _____ How far from hookup _____

Type of water_____

Is electric power available ____How far from hookup _____
Electric power available—check below
    120/208, 3 phrase, 60 cycle, 4 wire, "Wye" _____
    120/240, 3 phrase, 69 cycle, 4 wire, "Delta"_____
    240, 3 phrase, 69 cycle, 3 wire _____
Will curb cuts be permitted every 70 feet_____
Maximum opening for each curb cut permitted _____
Is septic system permitted_____If yes, proof must be submitted.
    Result of percolation test attached _____
    Is approval required by health dept. or governmental body __
    Is a plot plan layout required _____

13. General information of area within 5 miles
Type of housing in area _____
Cost bracket is between $_____and $ _____
Were homes built in the last 20 years _____
Are homes well maintained _____
Average persons per home____Average income per home____
Population within 1 mile____2 miles____3 miles _____
4 miles____5 miles____
Population of city or town _____
Population of city and suburbs _____

Attach the following:
- City map showing location, business activity
- Schools
- Pictures of area and site—explain on book of pictures detail shown.
- Plot or survey of site.
- Chamber of commerce information and data that are available.

FOR OFFICE USE ONLY

Source of location_____
Referral _____
Date, 1st field trip_____
Results_____
_____
Date, 2d field trip _____

SITE SELECTION

Results_____

_____

Date, 3d field trip _____
Results_____

_____

Date, engineer's inspection _____

_____

Results_____

_____

_____

INFORMATION TO BE OBTAINED AT CITY HALL AND PUBLIC SERVICE COMPANIES

1. What is the existing zoning _____
    Under existing zoning, can a self-service, drive-in restaurant be
    built _____
    Remarks _____
    Verified by Mr., Zoning Department, City Hall _____

2. Where is the water line _____Show on diagram
    In front of property _____
    Across the street from property _____
    In the middle of the street _____
    _____feet away _____
    Can we hook up to it _____
    Verified by Mr. _____, Water Department, City Hall

    _____

3. Where is the sanitary sewer_____Show on diagram
    In front of property _____
    Across the street from property _____
    In the middle of the street _____
    Verified by Mr. _____, Sewer Department, City Hall

    _____

4. Where is the natural gas line _____
    In front of property _____
    Across the street from property_____

_____feet away. Cost, if any, to bring to property_____

Verified by Mr., Gas Company _____

5. Where is the three-phase wiring _____

In front of property _____

Across the street from property _____

_____feet away. Cost, if any, to bring to property_____

Verified by Mr. _____, Electric Company _____

6. Can we obtain a permit to break curbs and install driveways —

Verified by Mr. _____, Street Department, City Hall

7. Can we erect a _____square-foot flashing sign on the parkway

Verified by Mr. _____, Electric Department, City Hall

DIAGRAM OF PLOT

Must be drawn in detail, showing directions and side of road: north, south, east, or west; proposed location of curb cuts or breaks already on property; number of curb cuts permitted; and sidewalks and who maintains. Show any trees, buildings, poles, fire hydrants, traffic lights, or bus stops. Attach to survey.

REQUIRED DOCUMENTS AND SITE REQUIREMENTS

1. Letter from realtor stating why site meets requirements.
2. Checklist completed.
3. Neighborhood map.
4. Plan or survey of the property.
5. Photographs—8 shots of site, land on each side, area across the street.
6. Lease offer.
7. Aerial photo, with site marked and 2-mile radius noted.
8. City map showing subject site, 2-mile radius circle, and all other committed rib cage locations.
9. Census tract study—2-mile radius.

Branchising Alternatives

A SUMMARY

1. **Leasing.** Continuing revenue is obtainable through the renting or leasing of structure, equipment, or other factors.

2. **Buying Office.** A buying office is an accepted, traditional entity. It offers a buying service for its affiliated members. As such, it receives the equivalent of an establishment fee and a continuing monthly fee. Also, in some instances, it may receive a designated percentage on purchases made under its auspices. How applicable is the buying office format to your type of business?

3. **Management Advisory Service.** Normally, when a company engages this type of service, they pay an initial "program" fee and a continuing advisory fee (or retainer). Such an arrangement is often characteristic of motels; a continuing per-room or per-occupancy fee is paid as a royalty to the parent organization. Another example is a boat-restaurant that cruises shorelines. The client in one instance became the operating manager on behalf of the investor group. The manager could be thought of as the general partner, and the investors, the limited partner.

4. **Consultant.** Most consultants receive an initial establishment or project fee and a continuing program-sustaining fee, which is usually equated to receiving a royalty. Often this is tied in with an added percentage of sales. Here again, there is possible applicability to your program by being a consultant to new or existing businesses.

5. **Condominium Approach.** As you know, the usual condominium is based on the purchase of component units with central management input and control. The management obtains continuing revenue for its services. One interesting example of an unusual condominium is a well-known camp ground. (The president attended one of our seminars.) In effect, the condominiums were its parking spaces; the management retained the facilities (swimming pool, food services, etc.). The management also undertook to rent unoccupied spaces in behalf of their owners and obtained a profit for this, too. In this instance, virtually no financing was required by the management; this was achieved through the unit sales. However, management retained enough substantial profit centers for itself to have substantial continuing earnings.

   Let's look at other condominium possibilities. For example, what if various craftspeople in the building field were converted into a condominium, e.g., home remodeling. Units could be sold to a plumber, a painter, a carpenter, an electrician, etc.

   There was another example which came up during a recent seminar. These people set up the equivalent of a condominium for the medical field offering a centralized reception laboratory, computerized billing, and other services.

   How is this applicable to you?

APP. A

6. **Direct Sales.** As previously discussed, this is a comparatively unknown field that has vast earnings potential. Over 200,000 direct salespersons are available throughout the United States and Canada. They will work on a commission basis, demonstrate what you have, and get right into the homes to do so. During recession times, this field is particularly effective.

7. **Partnership Concept.** There are many ways in which this can be applied. You (as the Branchisor) can be the general partner, and the investor (as the Branchisee) can be the limited partner. And vice versa. As the general partner you may also operate the project for a designated management fee, e.g., 15 percent.

8. **Existing Corporation Concept.** Sell shares in your existing corporation, e.g. 49 percent, which leaves you with a controlling interest. The corporate bylaws can spell out the terms of your respective relationships. Frequently, the Branchisee is allotted a designated compensation as operating manager for the corporation.

    In some instances the Branchisee (usually a younger person who can't afford to meet the required investment) will invest in as little as 10 percent of the stock, and he will be given the opportunity to buy in (at a designated price) until he has a majority interest. We had done this in one instance for a drugstore chain. Each store required an investment of $300,000. Seminars were conducted that brought together pharmacists (who had very little money but yet were the vitally needed worker-managers) and financiers (who sought the tax benefits of this type of investment). Each pharmacist invested 10 percent, received a salary, and was given the opportunity to obtain more shares—through purchases and bonuses—to keep adding to his equity interest.

9. **Sales Agency Concept.** One example was that of a company in the furniture field. The Branchisee committed itself to store rental and personnel, and the Branchisor supplied furniture needed for store display. All orders were filled by the Branchisor, and the Branchisee received a designated commission check each week.

10. **Sell Training.** This concept is similar to the usual "school concept," for example, travel schools, etc. It's also similar to H&R Block's concept whereby they charge a $100-tuition fee for training. These thousands of trainees provided an inventory of skilled workers able to help out H&R Block franchisees during the peak season.

    This training concept also has possible residual benefits, relative to furnishing products and services on a continuing basis not normally available through other sources.

11. **Subleasing Concept.** Many Branchisors (including McDonald's) assess a percentage override and rental, as much as 12 percent in some cases. In other instances a minimum rent plus sales percentage is required. This often brings earnings beyond usual royalties. And as we know, the usual lease agreement can be highly restrictive, much more so than the usual franchise agreement. In the instances of Firestone and Goodyear franchises, the lease had also been an important factor.

12. **The Vending Concept.** Many types of products are vendable. The successful Snap-on Tools business is in effect "vending on a vehicle." Often this can be linked to buying back nonpurchased merchandise.

13. **Using Your Financial Resources.** Do you have maximum bonding capacity? Do you have management skills, and an outstanding reputation in your field? You can profitably Branchise this as a commodity. There was the instance of a client of ours in the construction field. This company had a bonding capacity of approximately $20 million and outstanding management skills that could practically guarantee net profits in a field which was notoriously poorly managed. The company also had an outstanding reputation: They had constructed multimillion-dollar government and other buildings. They thus upgraded the smaller builder, e.g., the one who only had a $500,000-bondable capacity, to be able to bid on the multimillion-dollar job (using the Branchisor's credentials) and to make an assured profit.

14. **Buy Piece of Business.** This plan enabled the entrepreneur to obtain with virtually no initial investment a 50 percent interest in each unit. The Branchisee (or operating manager) in effect invested for the training, basic salary, and potential bonuses. As we all know, this concept has been highly successful. At one point there was a waiting list of prospective managers and investors.

15. **Trademarks, Patents, and Techniques.** These are assets. They are salable or rentable. Consider how they can apply to your assets.

16. **The ESOP Plan.** Through this plan, employees contribute capital to a business by buying shares. The company obtains 100 percent dollars in exchange for 50 percent tax dollars.

Using Census Data to Select a Site

SUMMARY*

In the crucial matter of selecting a location for your business, many factors must be weighed. A frequently overlooked source of valuable information is the U.S. Census. In addition to nationwide statistics, reports are available for every city, town, or village. For cities of 50,000 or more inhabitants, material has been tabulated for census tracts—small areas with an average population of about four to five thousand. Such summary information is available for the entire metropolitan area in which such a city is located, as well as for individual blocks within the city.

It is up to you to obtain the pertinent data and use your own judgment in interpreting it in terms of your particular business. The effort is likely to increase your store's chances for success.

SCOPE OF SITE ANALYSIS

No decision is more important to a retail store owner than selecting the location for his business. Even if you have ample financial resources and above-average managerial skills, they can't offset the handicap of a poor location. Moving is costly. Legal complications of a lease can be difficult to untangle—not to mention other location-related problems that could arise. Clearly, your careful examination of alternative sites is a worthwhile endeavor. By studying the relevant Bureau of the Census reports, you can develop valuable insights about the characteristics of prospective customers as well as knowledge about the economic strengths and weaknesses of your trading area.

Every store has a trading area—in other words, the geographic region from which it draws its potential customers. Data for trading areas, regardless of size, generally can be assembled by combining a number of census tract tables. These may be your best single source of information. However, if you are going to make a complete store location analysis, they should be supplemented with other material.

Unlike a manufacturing operation which usually can ship its products elsewhere, the potential business of a retail store is limited to its trading area. The primary area can range from a number of blocks for a small neighborhood store to a 35-mile radius for a store located in a large shopping center.

If you are the prospective owner of a single store, your main concern will be the factors that

*This is a reprint of "Using Census Data to Select a Store Site," by Louis H. Vorzimer, Small Business Administration, Small Marketers Aid No. 154, 1975.

have direct relevance to your store's trading area. Far too many small retailers select a store site by chance. (In fact, the most common reason given is "noticed vacancy.") Their high turnover rate would be considerably lower had they analyzed in advance the trading area's population characteristics, housing characteristics, nature and quality of competition, traffic count, and accessibility. It is also of fundamental importance to determine total consumer purchasing power and the store's expected share of this total. Each location analysis must be done on a custom study basis, focusing on your particular line of retailing. Answers to questions like the following can be found in the census reports.

—How many persons or families are there in the trading area and how has this changed over time?

—Where do they work?

—How many young or old persons are there, how many children or teenagers?

—How many families with small children or with teenagers?

—How many one-person households, how many small or large families?

—What is the income of the families or individuals?

—What do they do for a living?

—Is the area an older established one or one where most residents are newcomers?

—How many families own their homes? How many rent?

—What is the value of the homes? What is the monthly rent?

—What is the age and quality of the homes?

—Do the homes have air conditioning; other appliances?

—How many of the families own an automobile? How many own two or more?

GEOGRAPHICAL BREAKDOWNS

The *Standard Metropolitan Statistical Area* (SMSA) geographical designation includes a county (or counties) containing a central city of at least 50,000 inhabitants, plus contiguous counties which are socially and economically integrated with the central county. In some cases, there may be twin cities with a total population of 50,000 or more (the smaller of the two cities with at least 15,000 people). There are 267 tracted standard SMSA's in the United States and Puerto Rico.

Census tracts are subdivisions of SMSA's. Large cities and adjacent areas have been divided for the purpose of showing comparable small area statistics. The average tract has about 4,000 to 5,000 residents. One report is published for each SMSA. It includes statistical information about each tract and also includes a map for reference. The information is based on the 1970 Census of Population and Housing. Altogether this amounts to some 34,000 tracts.

While the census tract usually constitutes a geographic unit small enough for a retail store location analysis, you may want to examine even smaller units. *Block statistics* within a census tract are available for urbanized areas. (An urbanized area for the 1970 Census consists of a central city or cities, as well as surrounding closely settled territory.) These reports by city blocks present data on general characteristics of housing and population for some 1.8 million blocks. Because these are such small geographic units, they provide less census information than the reports for census tracts. You may not be interested in any specific block as such, but you can combine blocks into special trading areas. Again, appropriate maps are included with block statistics. (A sample from a page of the block statistics is shown further on to give you an idea of how they appear in the census reports.)

USING CENSUS TRACTS

In the census tract reports the statistical information is arranged in tables for the entire population of the specific area. In addition, there are tables for minority groups. However, information of this type is available only for tracts that have a population of 400 or more for the particular minority group.

For purposes of discussion, this *Aid* focuses on two census tracts from the 1970 Tacoma, Washington, SMSA. Tracts 718.02 and 719.02 are compared in order to point out important differences that exist even though each has about the same size population and they are closely located geographically. For convenience, the former is referred to as Tract A and the latter as Tract B. Each will be considered to be the entire trading area for prospective lines of retailing. Although the characteristics extracted for this *Aid* are only a partial listing, they are representative of information available in census tract reports. A number of the selected characteristics are analyzed on an individual basis for the purpose of illustration. In practice, the interrelationship of all characteristics must be given consideration.

Table B-1—General Characteristics of the Population

Race   Comparing Tract A and Tract B reveals that Tract A has a higher percent Negro population, 7.9 percent versus 1.0 percent in Tract B. Since Tract A has more than 400 Negroes, separate statistics for the black population are available in the tract report.

Age by Sex—Male, All Ages   Even though the total population is about the same for the two tracts, significant differences exist in a number of male age groups. For the under 5 years group, Tract A has more than twice as many as Tract B. The presence of this group could be of importance for a Children's Wear Store. The situation is reversed for the 15 to 19 years group; Tract B has a significantly larger number. A sizable group of teenagers could be of consequence for a Record Store, since they are heavy purchasers of records. Other major male age group population differences could have relevance for other lines of retailing.

The population for "Female, all ages" and other General Characteristics of the Population are not shown in this *Aid* but are available in the actual census tracts report.

Table B-2—Social Characteristics of the Population

Nativity, Parentage, and Country of Origin.   There are no major differences between the two tracts. Most of the residents in each are native born. Tract A has a greater proportion of foreign origin but the number is not significantly large. When the population of foreign stock is sizable, it is a good idea to research the customs and traditions of the group or groups to anticipate their reaction to products of a particular line of business. You might even consider a business that would cater to ethnic preferences.

Years of School Completed—Persons, 25 Years Old and Over   Tract B has more people over 25 years. They have more education, as shown by the higher percentage of high school graduates and the number of college educated.

Table B-3—Labor Force Characteristics of the Population

Occupation—Total Employed, 16 Years Old and Over   In Tract B, a much larger number of persons over 15 are employed. Tract B also has more people in the occupations that require more education. Particular reference is made to "Professional, technical, and kindred workers" and to "Managers and administrators, except farm."

USING CENSUS DATA TO SELECT A SITE   209

TABLE B-1 General Characteristics of the Population

	Tract A	Tract B
Race		
All persons	**5 649**	**5 636**
White	4 684	5 468
Negro	448	58
Percent Negro.	7.9	1.0
Age by Sex		
Male, all ages	**2 795**	**2 754**
Under 5 years	353	168
3 and 4 years.	102	72
5 to 9 years	237	211
5 years.	47	33
6 years.	47	42
10 to 14 years	207	327
14 years	30	82
15 to 19 years	186	315
15 years.	31	70
16 years.	35	82
17 years.	35	75
18 years.	33	64
19 years.	52	24
20 to 24 years	751	222
20 years.	126	38
21 years.	179	34
25 to 34 years	445	280
35 to 44 years	241	341
45 to 54 years	201	445
55 to 59 years	61	154
60 to 64 years	48	108
65 to 74 years	40	128
75 years and over	25	55

TABLE B-2 Social Characteristics of the Population

	Tract A	Tract B
Nativity, Parentage, & Country of Origin		
All persons	**5 649**	**5 636**
Native of native parentage	4 393	4 465
Native of foreign or mixed parentage	809	884
Foreign born	447	287
Foreign stock	**1 256**	**1 171**
United Kingdom	103	95
Ireland (Eire)	—	16
Sweden	—	91
Germany	218	124
Poland	29	22
Czechoslovakia	7	6
Austria	18	9
Hungary	—	14
U.S.S.R.	13	23
Italy	7	22
Canada	121	209
Mexico	37	21
Cuba	—	—
Other America	17	—
All other and not reported	686	519
Persons of Spanish language	210	112
Other persons of Spanish surname	—	—
Persons of Spanish mother tongue	141	38
Persons of Puerto Rican birth or parentage	14	—
Years of School Completed		
Persons, 25 years old and over	**2 120**	**3 201**
No school years completed	13	4
Elementary: 1 to 4 years	21	5
5 to 7 years	89	61
8 years	250	146
High School: 1 to 3 years	412	357
4 years	983	1 086
College: 1 to 3 years	210	729
4 years or more	142	813
Median school years completed	12.3	12.9
Percent high school graduates	63.0	82.1

TABLE B-3 Labor Force Characteristics of the Population

	Tract A	Tract B
Occupation		
Total employed, 16 years old and over	1 479	2 234
Professional, technical, and kindred workers	152	505
Health workers	71	91
Teachers, elementary and secondary schools	26	116
Managers and administrators, except farm	67	427
Salaried	61	367
Self-employed in retail trade	6	28
Sales workers	80	247
Retail trade	69	109
Clerical and kindred workers	365	340
Craftsmen, foremen, and kindred workers	135	179
Construction craftsmen	45	58
Mechanics and repairmen	34	47
Operatives, except transport	146	122
Transport equipment operatives	22	73
Laborers, except farm	134	95
Farm workers	5	—
Service workers	347	211
Cleaning and food service workers	203	110
Protective service workers	16	10
Personal and health service workers	119	88
Private household workers	26	35

Table B-4—Income Characteristics of the Population

Income in 1969 of Families and Unrelated Individuals Tract B is stronger in the higher income groups, while Tract A has a high concentration of income in the under $8,000 groups. In choosing a location, the median income figure is more significant than the average income. Note that Tract B has a median income for "All families" of $14,094 against Tract A's median income of $6,423.

The term "median" is best explained by example. Assume that nine people have the following incomes:

$2,500	$4,100	$8,400
2,700	> 5,300 <	10,300
3,600	5,800	15,600

In this example, the middle, or median, item is the fifth. Four figures are higher and four figures are lower.

Implications of Education, Occupation, and Income

The three characteristics of education, occupation, and income have a strong interrelationship. Occupation is closely aligned with education, and higher income is generally associated with college graduates. Therefore, you would expect a tract with a high percent of college graduates to have a population with higher level jobs and higher income. The characteristics of Tract B bear this out.

212

TABLE B-4 Income Characteristics of the Population

	Tract A	Tract B
Income in 1969 of Families and Unrelated individuals		
All families	1 718	1 582
Less than $1,000.	88	25
$1,000 to $1,999	59	20
$2,000 to $2,999	119	30
$3,000 to $3,999	199	20
$4,000 to $4,999	174	32
$5,000 to $5,999	143	36
$6,000 to $6,999	182	49
$7,000 to $7,999	170	30
$8,000 to $8,999	119	125
$9,000 to $9,999	96	92
$10,000 to $11,999	131	168
$12,000 to $14,999	119	235
$15,000 to $24,999	109	381
$25,000 to $49,999	—	239
$50,000 or more.	10	100
Median income	$6 423	$14 094
Mean income	$7 640	$18 568
Families and unrelated individuals	2 215	1 948
Median income.	$6 077	$12 508
Mean income	$6 981	$16 420
Unrelated individuals	497	366
Median income	$5 056	$5 394
Mean income	$4 703	$7 135

The background of the group mentioned above could lead to certain buying habits and patterns. It is difficult to say whether a college graduate buys an item because of his education or because of his income. Nevertheless, it is probably true that persons with the same income but with variations in educational background would form separate market segments for many products.

Low income is a limiting factor for the purchase of products beyond the necessities. While expanded consumer credit has, to some extent, augmented the purchasing power of low income groups, the higher income groups constitute a better market for luxury or costly products. Upper income households account for disproportionately large shares of total spending for such product categories as home furnishings, equipment, and appliances. This also applies to alcoholic beverage, automotive products, recreation, and clothing.

The highest income market is made up of college graduates from the occupational groups of "Professional, technical, and kindred workers" and "Managers and administrators, except farm" who are in the 35 to 54 age groups. The trend toward an increasing number of college graduates each year should create greater demand for art, books, travel, and cultural activities.

Table B-5—Occupancy, Utilization, and Financial Characteristics of Housing Units

Value—Specified Owner Occupied Units   Tract B has three times as many owner occupied units. The median value of the owner occupied units is $27,100 compared to $13,800

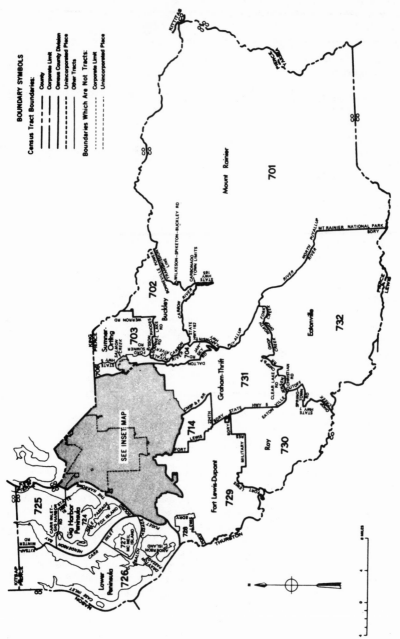

Figure B-1 A portion of the Tract A block statistics as they appear on a page of the actual census material.

214   BRANCHISING

TABLE B-5 Occupancy, Utilization, and Financial Characteristics of Housing Units

	Tract A	Tract B
All housing units	2 263	1 929
Value		
Specified owner occupied units[1]	429	1 341
Less than $5,000.	5	—
$5,000 to $7,499	15	7
$7,500 to $9,999	44	15
$10,000 to $14,999	207	89
$15,000 to $19,999	103	275
$20,000 to $24,999	29	237
$25,000 to $34,999	13	223
$35,000 to $49,999	4	192
$50,000 or more.	9	303
Median	$13 800	$27 100
Contract Rent		
Specified renter occupied units[2]	1 442	486
Less than $30.	6	5
$30 to $39	6	1
$40 to $59	24	11
$60 to $79	80	17
$80 to $99	244	65
$100 to $149	884	230
$150 to $199	164	80
$200 to $249	3	28
$250 or more	1	29
No cash rent.	30	20
Median	$121	$131

[1]Limited to one-family homes on less than 10 acres and no business on property.
[2]Excludes one-family homes on 10 acres or more.

for Tract A. This may have some relevance for purchasers of lawn mowers and garden equipment, hardware supplies, outdoor furniture, and many home maintenance items. For retailers of these products, Tract B is a much better location.

Contract Rent—Specified Renter Occupied Units Tract A has over three times as many renter units. There is little difference in the median rent of the two tracts. The renters generally live in multiple dwellings where space is usually more limited than in owner occupied units. This suggests a market for retailers of portable or smaller models of such items as washing machines and dryers, counter height freezers, and other items for which space is a problem.

Table B-6—Structural, Equipment, and Financial Characteristics of Housing Units

Heating Equipment Tract B has many more warm air furnaces. For a retailer selling this type of equipment, replacement and repair opportunities would be much better in Tract B than Tract A. In Tract A there is a much greater number of built-in electric units. This number is out of proportion to other regions in the United States. You should always investigate items that cannot be readily accounted for. In this case, the unusually large number of built-in electric units is due to the region's relatively low-cost electric power.

Basement   Tract B has many basements, while the reverse is true for Tract A. This indicates space availability, especially for power tools and hardware which are normally used and stored in basements and for furnishings and recreational equipment which are used in a finished basement.

Automobiles Available   Tract B not only has the higher total number of automobiles, it has many more units with two, three, or more automobiles. This coincides with the higher income of the tract and could suggest a better market for luxury and specialty products.

Block Statistics on Housing Units and Population

An example of characteristics by blocks appears on the following page. It shows how detailed a breakdown you can get. The sample reproduced was taken from the block statistics for Tract A.

CENSUS OF BUSINESS: RETAIL TRADE

The Census of Business is taken every 5 years and published in the years ending in 2 and 7—for example, 1967 and 1972. It contains nationwide statistics on retail, wholesale, and selected service trade establishments. The section on Retail Trade contains information such as the number of retail establishments, retail sales, number of paid employees, and payroll by kinds of business. The data are compiled by county, by SMSA, by cities over 2,500 population, and by *central business districts* (CBD's). They are not tabulated by tract. A CBD is an area of very high land valuation, characterized by dense concentration of retail stores, offices, theatres, hotels, and service businesses. You will find a CBD in most cities with a population of 100,000 or more.

Statistics for *major retail centers* (MRC's) are also published but usually in less detail than for the other statistical areas. An MRC is a concentration of retail stores, having at least $5 million

TABLE B-6   Structural, Equipment, and Financial Characteristics of Housing Units

	Tract A	Tract B
Heating Equipment		
Steam or hot water	23	206
Warm air furnace	394	1 132
Built-in electric units	1 209	296
Floor, wall, or pipeless furnace	105	101
Other means or not heated	532	194
Basement		
All units with basement	81	732
One-family houses with basement	64	673
Automobiles Available		
1	1 374	727
2	417	890
3 or more	109	241
None	190	6

Blocks Within Census Tracts

(Data exclude vacant seasonal and vacant migratory housing units. For minimum base for derived figures (percent, average, etc.) and meaning of symbols, see text)

		Percent of total population				Year-round housing units				Occupied housing units														
								Units in—		Owner					Renter					1.01 or more persons per room				
	Total population	Negro	In group quarters	Under 18 years	62 years and over	Total	Lacking some or all plumbing facilities	One-unit structures	Structures of 10 or more units	Total	Lacking some or all plumbing facilities	Average number of rooms	Average value (dollars)	Percent Negro	Total	Lacking some or all plumbing facilities	Average number of rooms	Average contract rent (dollars)	Percent Negro	Total	With all plumbing facilities	One-person households	With female head of family	With roomers, boarders, or lodgers
625	24	–	–	33	13	7	–	7	–	5	–	5.0	17300	–	2	...	...	...	–	2	2	1	–	–
626	54	–	–	32	6	22	–	15	5	7	–	6.1	21300	–	14	–	2.8	79	–	2	2	4	3	1
627	93	–	–	3	7	55	–	8	44	4	...	...	...	–	49	–	3.0	135	–	1	1	18	–	1
628	12	–	–	25	42	5	–	5	–	5	–	4.8	17500	–	–	–	–	–	–	–	–	1	–	–
629	11	–	–	9	–	5	–	5	–	5	–	5.2	15000	–	–	–	–	–	–	–	–	–	–	–
630	18	–	–	28	11	7	–	7	–	5	–	6.0	14800	–	2	...	...	...	–	–	–	1	–	–
631	2	...	...	...	...	1	...	...	...	...	...	...	...	...	...	...	...	...	...	...	...	...	...	...
632	36	–	–	14	42	24	3	4	–	21	2	2.9	...	–	2	...	...	...	–	1	1	13	1	–
718.02	5649	8	–	32	3	2263	9	898	714	639	6	4.7	15400	7	1451	3	3.7	121	8	163	163	306	213	32
102	36	8	–	33	8	12	1	12	–	9	1	5.4	16000	11	2	...	...	...	...	2	2	2	1	1
103	44	41	–	52	–	11	–	11	–	10	–	6.3	21400	40	1	...	...	...	...	1	1	–	1	–
104	18	6	–	17	28	10	–	6	–	2	...	...	...	...	7	–	3.9	99	14	–	–	3	2	1
105	129	1	–	36	1	44	–	17	–	13	–	6.4	26900	–	31	–	3.6	116	3	2	2	5	9	–
106	36	8	–	31	17	17	–	10	–	9	–	4.2	13800	–	6	–	4.0	102	–	–	–	4	1	–
107	504	14	–	35	5	191	–	67	51	84	–	4.6	13300	5	98	–	3.4	110	18	18	18	31	22	5
108	72	4	–	42	7	20	–	20	–	12	–	5.3	11700	8	7	–	4.4	100	14	3	3	1	3	–
109	85	11	–	46	–	27	–	27	–	15	–	4.3	15200	20	9	–	5.1	101	–	3	3	–	5	–
201	74	7	–	46	4	17	–	16	–	9	–	5.1	11500	11	8	–	4.8	118	13	3	3	–	3	–
202	85	4	–	38	4	29	–	28	–	20	–	5.5	14300	–	8	–	4.8	123	13	3	3	3	6	–
203	10	–	–	30	10	7	–	6	–	–	–	–	–	–	4	...	...	...	–	...	...	...	...	...
204	50	18	–	26	8	18	–	17	1	13	–	4.8	14300	15	5	–	4.6	123	–	2	2	2	–	1
205	59	7	–	42	2	20	–	20	–	10	–	5.2	12800	10	7	–	4.6	91	29	3	3	3	1	–
206	102	10	–	44	–	27	–	26	–	16	–	4.2	12800	13	11	–	4.5	98	9	4	4	3	4	1
207	109	16	–	44	3	37	–	36	–	23	–	4.3	12800	4	9	–	4.6	94	22	6	6	6	4	–
208	176	9	–	49	2	48	–	47		22	–	4.6	12600	9	26	–	4.5	101	12	11	11	4	14	1
209	79	9	–	52	5	22	–	21	–	13	–	4.8	11600	8	7	–	4.9	121	–	5	5	1	4	–
210	85	14	–	34	2	25	1	24	–	15	1	4.8	12400	20	10	–	5.0	105	20	3	3	4	3	–
211	73	22	–	49	3	19	–	19	–	13	–	5.8	14300	8	6	–	5.0	128	50	3	3	1	5	–

Figure B-2

in retail sales and at least 10 retail establishments, one of which is a department store. It may include not only a planned shopping center but the older string streets and community developments.

Both the MRC and the CBD are located inside the SMSA; the MRC is outside the CBD. Census data and accompanying maps showing CBD and MRC boundaries can be found in many public libraries in the *Major Retail Centers Series* (RC72-C—1 to 50). There is one for each State.

EVALUATING CENSUS INFORMATION

The information you glean from studying the Bureau of the Census reports must be pulled together to provide you with a clear picture. When you have carefully organized the data you have gathered, you will be able to see the interrelationship of the tabulated characteristics. Your own judgment as to what material is relevant for your study is a key factor. Since much of the data is based on the U.S. Census taken every 10 years, the information becomes somewhat dated toward the end of the decade. Even so, with some exceptions, it still provides a relative measurement among trading areas.

While the information from census reports is of inestimable value, you should supplement it with on-the-spot observations of your own. Walk or ride through a prospective trading area. Observe the people and the competition. Compile counts of pedestrian and automobile traffic. You can get statistics for traffic information from a State agency. (For the name of the agency, consult your nearest SBA field office.) The time you spend on store location analysis will be well rewarded by your store's success and share of business in its trading area.

OBTAINING BUREAU OF THE CENSUS PUBLICATIONS

Bureau of the Census publications are available for reference purposes at many libraries. They also may be used or purchased at the U.S. Department of Commerce district offices, which are located in 43 major cities. In addition, some 700 "cooperative offices" run by local chambers of commerce also offer Bureau of the Census leaflets and other informative printed matter. Nearly all of the publications may be purchased from the Superintendent of Documents, U.S. Government Printing Office, Washington, D.C. 20402; some publications may be obtained only from the Bureau of the Census. For an order form listing tract and block reports, write to the Publications Distribution Section, Bureau of the Census, Social and Economic Statistics Administration, Washington, D.C. 20233.

FOR FURTHER INFORMATION

[Individuals] who wish to further explore the subject of using census data may consult the references shown below. The list is necessarily brief. No slight is intended toward authors whose works are not mentioned.

Effective Business Relocation by William N. Kinnard, Jr., and Stephen D. Messner. 1970. D. C. Heath and Company, 2700 North Rechardt Ave., Indianapolis, Ind. 46219. $13.50.

Survey of Buying Power. Published annually in June by Sales Management, Inc., 630 Third Ave., New York, N.Y. 10017. $25.00.

MINI-GUIDE *to the 1972 Economic Censuses.* November 1973. For sale by Publications Distribution Section, Publication Services Division, Social and Economic Statistics Administration, Washington, D.C. 20233. Price $1.00.

Bureau of the Census Guide to Programs and Publications, 1973. Available from the Superintendent of Documents, Washington, D.C. 20402 and from district offices of the Department of Commerce.

Small Business Bibliography No. 10, "Retailing." Free from your nearest SBA office or from the U.S. Small Business Administration, Washington, D.C. 20416.

Small Marketers Aid No. 152, "Using a Traffic Study to Select a Retail Site." Free from your nearest SBA office or from the U.S. Small Business Administration, Washington, D.C. 20416.

Index

Record-keeping:
  of advertising results, 107–108
  of phone calls, 108, 109
  proper, 164–174
  value of break-even chart dependent on sound, 177
Recruitment, 76, 103–113
  example of Branching sales procedures for, 108–113
  hypothetical branch operator recruitment projections, 128–133
  of master and regional Branchisees in international Branching, 49
  and qualification criteria for associates, 103–104
  systems, procedures, and forms for, 104–108
  use of media for locating prospective Branchisees, 104
Red Carpet (firm), 40
Reference numbers, function of, 105–106
Regional Branchisees, recruitment of, 49
Regional seminars for training purposes, 117
Related products, promotion with addition of, 149–150
Rent-it departments, 149
Rental plans, dealer, 30
Resident directors in international Branching, 47
Retail sales, franchised, 18–19
Retail trade, census of, 216–218
Robbery, defined, 190
Robert Hall (firm), 11
Rockwood Industries (firm), 24
Roving vehicles, preopening promotion with, 160
Royalty and licensing agreements, 20
Rural Electrification Administration, 82

Salaried employees:
  entrepreneurial management vs., 1, 8
  financial ratios to determine wages of, 180
Sales:
  direct, as option, 28–29, 204
  examples of procedures for Branching, 108–113
  franchised retail, 18–19
  manual of, 75
  of partial profits, 40–41
  presentation book for, 75
  sales activity sheets, 108, 110, 111
  sales backup by home office personnel, 88
  of shares of stock as option, 37–38
Sales agency, commission, as option, 42, 204
Sales representatives, independent, as option, 38–39

Salesman's Opportunity (magazine), 29
Salespeople from nonprofit organizations, promotion with, 149
Sambos (firm), 10
Sears, Roebuck & Co., 10, 24, 29, 148
Secretaries, branch, job descriptions for, 74
Self-activity programs:
  self-check activity forms, 86–87
  self-inspection checklist programs, 90–92
Sell training as option, 19, 204
Selling of systems, 152
Seminars:
  to attract customers, 151
  district and regional, for training purposes, 117
Share(s) of stock:
  net profit per, defined, 43
  selling, as option, 37–38
Sherman Antitrust Act (1890), 20
Short-term financing, 81
Signs:
  preopening, 159
  stand-up promotional, 148
Site selection, 195–201
  checklists for, 196–201
  difficulty in obtaining good sites as influential factor, 14
  and evaluation of marketing territory, 195
  using census data, 207–219
Size of qualification forms, 134
Sky Chefs' (firm), quality control program of, 93–101
Small Business Administration (SBA), 218, 219
  loans from, 58, 82
Small Business Association, 167
Small Business Bibliography No. 10 ("Retailing"), 219
Small Business Investment Company (SBICs), loans from, 58, 78–79, 82
Small Marketers Aid No. 152 ("Using a Traffic Study to Select a Retail Site"), 219
Snap-on Tools (firm), 150, 204
Specialty Salesman (magazine), 29
Spontaneous phone calls, supervision with, 87
Stand-up signs, promotional, 148
Standard Metropolitan Statistical Areas (SMSAs), 208, 209, 216, 218
Standard Oil Company of New Jersey, 11
Start-up profit sharing plan, 43
Stock [see Share(s) of stock]
Store promotion, individual, by wholesalers, 33
Straight commercial loans, 78